The Determined Lady Elizabeth

JOAN DEAN

Columbus, Ohio

Special Thanks to my family and friends for their patience
and encouragement.

The Determined Lady Elizabeth

Published by Gatekeeper Press
2167 Stringtown Rd, Suite 109
Columbus, OH 43123-2989
www.GatekeeperPress.com

Library of Congress Control Number: t/k

ISBN (hardcover): t/k
ISBN (paperback): t/k
eISBN: t/k

Table of Contents

Introduction

A fine carriage, drawn by four black, well-matched horses, galloping together, is moving quickly along a well-groomed country road. The City of London has given way to smaller towns, and now, a beautiful, open hill of lush land is upon them. Large, older trees, of silver birch, oak, and black alder decorate the landscape for as far as can be seen. Some trees are in small groups, some stand alone, and some are together in such thick, expansive settings that treetops blot out the sun, when passing underneath. This landscape is known to the passenger, who is quietly reading. Dressed in a fashionable silk and lace gown, wearing pearl drop earrings, and covered with a hooded cloak of damask blue and silver flowered print, tells the world that she is of the nobility. She is twenty years old and has left the court of King George I and Queen Sophia Dorothea, where she was one of the Maids of Honor at the household of Princess Caroline, The Princess of Wales. She was given permission to leave court, for the time being, to be with her ailing father. She is not happy that he is ailing; but, she is happy to be able to spend more time with him.

Chapter 1

Lord Addington is seated in a comfortable chair, in his bedroom. His dog, Leo, older now, but always at his side, takes the opportunity to rest, while the Lord scratches his ear.

After checking him over, Dr. Brown says, "William, you and I have known each other for many years. I am not going to give you some fancy explanation. You know you had a small stroke yesterday; you should be in a hospital. I have given you advice before, and you did not follow it then; I am expecting you will not follow it now, either."

"Your heart is not as strong since Lady Agnes passed away. If you continue working like this, I will not be coming here many more times! And speaking of that, I will be going to my niece's wedding in Northumberland in two weeks, and will be gone for about two months. I will be visiting family, as well."

A once strong, healthy man in his later fifties, Lord Addington, jokingly replies, "What! You are leaving me alone…in my weakened condition?"

Dr. Brown, sighing and looking Heavenward, states, "No, I am not. Another doctor, a Doctor Robert Barnett, will be covering my patient's care for me. He is younger; he graduated from Oxford University; he studied with some fine professors and physicians. He has some new ideas about medicine, too. Now, for goodness sake, William, do not give him any trouble. I expect to find you, still here, when I get back."

His Lordship says, "I am not promising anything!"

Smiling, because of their friendship, Dr. Brown simply remarks, "Take care, William."

Leaving the room, he heads downstairs. Lewis, the long-time butler, meets him by the front door. Going out to his carriage, he drives away.

Lord Addington tells his valet, "Remember our 'arrangement.' No talk about doctors, to anyone." The valet responds, "What doctor, your Lordship?" Lord Addington smiles.

Inside the coach, the young woman puts down her book. Looking out the window, she notices the change in landscape and smiles. Home is nearby!

Finally, the coach pulls up to the front of her home, Addington Manor. A footman appears and holds the reins while the young lady emerges. Her luggage is removed, and Lewis is at the door, coming to greet her. "Lady Elizabeth, how good to see you!"

Relieved, she says, "Oh, it is so good to be home. I have missed everyone, so much!"

She bends her head a little closer. "Tell me, how are things with my father? The Viscount wrote me that he had been ill."

Lewis responds, "Well, that is something you will have to discuss with your father, my Lady."

Lady Elizabeth says quietly, "Let us keep this between ourselves, for now. But, you will let me know if there is any reason for concern. Just do not tell him!" the butler affirms, "As you wish."

Removing her hat and cloak in the foyer, Lady Elizabeth hurries into the library. Leo, who had been dozing in front of the fireplace, gets up and goes to greet her as soon as he sees her at the open door. Returning his greeting, she pats his head.

Her father smiles broadly; his joy at seeing her is evident. They embrace. Eagerly she settles herself in the chair across from her father, who is seated with a small blanket across his lap.

She declares, "I cannot tell you how good it feels to be home! We have a lot of catching up to do. And I want to know everything that is going on here."

Lord Addington, questioningly, says, "But, I thought you were enjoying court. Not many young ladies have a chance to be where there are wonderful parties and interesting people. Was there something you would like me to do?"

Lady Elizabeth explains, "I liked it in the beginning; but I grew bored with court life. And, after two years of being around so many people who worry about unimportant things, I realized that I did not really fit in. I began to miss my family greatly. So, I made up a story. I told the Princess of Wales that you needed me here. I asked her permission to leave court and Princess Caroline gave it. When I left, I pretended to be sorry; but I confess this to you, I was not sorry at all! I hope you are not angry."

Lord Addington divulges, "How could I be angry, if it means I get to see my own daughter? Do not tell Princess Caroline; but I am glad to have you back. This will be our secret."

The library becomes filled with the quiet contentment of two people who are at peace with the world.

Chapter 2

The next morning, Elizabeth and her father arrive on the staircase, at the same time, and walk, together down to breakfast. Never far from his master, Leo follows them, happily wagging his tail. Watching her father carefully, she notices that it is difficult for him to maneuver some of the steps unaided. She walks a little slower.

Elizabeth makes a promise to herself that she will have to learn everything she can about running the manor if her father is to be free from stress. Then, she will begin taking over the responsibilities, as quickly and quietly as possible. But first, she must talk with the agent. After that, she will know what to tell her brother.

After breakfast, Lady Elizabeth asks Lewis, "Where would I be able to find Wrede at this hour?"

The butler tells her, "He is usually in the agent's office. I will have him come to the house."

Lady Elizabeth says quickly, "No! I will go to see him. If anyone asks, I have gone out."

Donning a hooded cloak, Lady Elizabeth walks over to the manor's offices, in search of the agent.

She enters the office where two people are working; seeing her, they stand and greet her enthusiastically.

The older man greets Lady Elizabeth warmly, "I was hoping to see you. Come in. We have a lot to go over, my Lady."

"Thank you, Wrede, " she says. He bids her to sit in the big chair at the table. As she removes her cloak, he brings out maps of the estate grounds and account books. Together, they go over the ledgers, and he gives an accounting of all assets and expenses. Hours pass by.

Wrede suggests that, sometime soon, they ride out and survey the land, properties, and the village. "I miss doing all this with your father. But, he has not been…well, as strong …" his voice trails off. Lady Elizabeth adds, "I want to be as much help to him as I can, while I can."

Wrede says, "I am not as strong as I once was, either. I shall be retiring, soon, too, my Lady!"

Lady Elizabeth declares, "Then, if you can promise not to leave before the year is over, with your help, I shall apply myself and be a quick learner. And thank you, Wrede, for your loyalty and good service all these years." He smiles, sheepishly.

Three Weeks Later

Lord Addington, upon seeing Lady Elizabeth, says, "My dear, I am glad to see you this morning. I have missed having breakfast with you. I am sure it is because you have been busy. Tell me what has taken so much of your time."

She responds, "Good morning, Father. I am glad to see you, as well! I have made a few trips into town. I am interested in seeing what changes have occurred and what new shops are available. I have also been spending time looking about the manor and countryside. So, I have missed a meal here and there. I am sorry, Father. I shall endeavor to spend more time with you."

Chapter 3

London, Berwick House, Home of the Earl of Berwick, Lord and Lady Berwick and their two daughters, Lady Pricilla, age twenty-three years, and Lady Margery, sixteen years.

From behind his library desk, Lord Berwick, with his wife present, starts to talk to his daughter, Lady Pricilla, "My dear, the reason your mother and I wanted to talk to you this morning is because we wanted to know how things between you and Viscount Shelbourne are progressing."

Lady Pricilla opens her mouth to respond; but, before she can, her father holds up his hand, "You see, there are circumstances of which you were not fully apprised. The time has come for us to share that information with you. We, your mother and I, naturally thought that when you went away to court you would find a suitable husband. After all, you are a very lovely young woman from a family with a small estate, but who also mixes with the 'ton regularly.

"That, however, did not happen. Now, you are twenty-three years old, and each year more young ladies will come out into society. It is important that you find, and settle on, a man of means fairly soon. Right now, we have money set aside for dowries for both you and your sister. If there would come a time when we would need to use some of those funds it could be disastrous for your future. And, if anything happens to me, neither your mother nor you girls will inherit this house. It will go to the next male heir, which is my brother's family. As town homes go, this one is not a grand scale, so he will likely choose to put you all out.

"My point is that you are seeing a young man who fits the profile perfectly. Viscount Shelborne is the right age, unattached, and is next in line to be the Earl of Addington. The family is certainly wealthy and, it seems, has many excellent connections. So, please try to make this work to your advantage. Your mother can help by explaining what kind of characteristics a man will actively look for in marrying. I am telling you this so you will know how to apply yourself to John's interests. We, for our part, will see to it that you have the fine gowns and accessories necessary to acquire such a match. I understand that he is calling on you, this afternoon. That is good. Keep me informed. You may go now."

Later that Day

Lady Pricilla is in her bedroom. Dressed in a fashionable new outfit, she is standing in front of her mirror and asks her mother and sister, "How do I look?" Looking pleased, her mother says "Your dress looks wonderful. It is perfect! What time is the Viscount calling?" Pricilla responds, "He is coming to call at 4:00 PM. So, he will be here soon. We are going to a new little shop in town. It serves coffee and has several new items made with sugar from the Caribbean. That is what he said. What is a *Caribbean*, anyway? I am hoping his interest will turn into something permanent, and we will go to wonderful balls and parties, instead of a coffee shop."

Margery asks, "Do you want him to call again?"

"I am certainly going to work to that end. Would you get that dog of yours out of here? How can I concentrate with that mongrel around?" Pricilla exclaims.

"You will do fine. Just do not appear too independent or too knowledgeable. Men do not like that. He must think that any ideas he has are wonderful. Now, wait here. He will be here any minute," her mother directs.

The Viscount's coach arrives. He enters the townhouse just as their butler opens the door. He nods politely. Lady Pricilla has timed her entrance. She starts to walk slowly down the staircase, just as he is looking up. She smiles sweetly at him.

"Lady Pricilla, good day to you!" He bows politely. "Good day to you, Viscount," Pricilla declares. Her maid hands her a cloak and they depart.

Chapter 4

Morning, Manor House,

Servants are working when they hear the sound of something drop on the floor.

The Lord's valet hurries back into the changing room, finding him on the floor; he is conscious, but unable to get up. The doctor is summoned as servants help him up

In a short time, a carriage swiftly pulls up to the front entrance. A man alights carrying a black bag.

His Lordship insists, "See that no one is on the upper gallery hallway; then, have him come up."

Lewis opens the door and guides the man upstairs, to His Lordship's bedroom.

Upon seeing the man, Lord Addington asks, "Who are you?"

Doctor Barnett replies, "I am a doctor. My name is Robert Barnett. I am treating the patients of Doctor Brown over the next several weeks, while he is away in Northumberland, at his niece's wedding. I think he mentioned that to you. Tell me, what happened to you?"

The Lord says, "Well, it is quite simple. One moment I was standing; then, I felt a sharp pain, my leg weakened, and I was on the floor! It is nothing, really."

"Ah, well I guess you have already made a diagnosis. Do you still need me?" the doctor says, smiling.

His Lordship, somewhat abashed, says, "You are here now; you might as well check things over, just to see if we agree," he says, teasingly. The doctor understands, and smiles.

Finding no harm done, the doctor concludes his visit and says, "Goodbye." In a whisper, the valet says to the doctor, "Ask Lewis to take you out through the side exit. He does not want anyone to know you were here."

Finding this only slightly unusual compared to some 'exits' a doctor must make, he is not upset.

A little later at Manor House

In the morning room, Elizabeth is looking out the window, toward the large park. She turns from the window and walks toward the table for breakfast. A copy of the newspaper is on the table. Her father expresses, "I do not know how printers can afford to put out a newspaper anymore, when the Tax Act has gone up so monstrously!"

Elizabeth says, "I do not know either; but I am glad they do. Otherwise, we shall not know even the half of what is going on!" She turns to him questioningly, "Was there someone here this morning? I thought I heard someone talking on the gallery when I was getting ready for breakfast."

His Lordship says, "I am sure it was just the servants moving about, my dear. Nothing for you to worry about! "

Elizabeth accepts this and says, "Speaking of what is going on, I am riding out later this morning; but I have some correspondences to take care of before then. And Lady Margaret Smith-Lawson's dinner party is tonight. I would be honored if you would accompany me," she states, sincerely.

"I would like nothing more, my dear. But, my affinity for large meals and dancing all night has diminished over the years. These days, I look forward to a light meal, a good book, and a fine brandy. But, please, give my regards to everyone, though."

"I have some paperwork to do, as well. His Lordship continues, "So, I shall see you this afternoon. And, Beth, take care while you are out riding…I mean it!" Elizabeth, smiling, says, "Of course!" She stands, ready to leave. Lord Addington looks up meaningfully, "Do not forget, I have seen how you ride." Smiling, she walks over to him and kisses him on the forehead, "I love you, too!"

Leaving the room shortly after his daughter, he moves slowly, wincing.

In the Foyer:

Elizabeth asks a servant, "Please, have Tom ready my horse. I will be riding out within the hour."

The servant girl, curtsying, says, "Yes, my Lady." Elizabeth goes upstairs to her room.

Meanwhile, Lord Addington, goes into his library, closes the door and tries to complete his paperwork.

Elizabeth, dressed in her riding outfit, approaches the stable door and sees that Blackfire is ready.

Reaching the large black horse, she begins stroking his neck, cooing, "How is our favorite horse doing?" Tom, the stable hand responds, "He has missed riding out with you, and he is ready to go! Nice to have you back, your Ladyship, " Tom smiles as he tips his hat.

She climbs up into saddle. "Thank you, Tom. I can always count on you."

Smiling, she turns the horse toward the open gate and rides off.

Chapter 5

In short order, Elizabeth is galloping across hills and dales, jumping over small streams, and riding through wooded areas. Miles from home, in wide open, grassy countryside, she spurs her horse up an embankment. As the horse reaches the top, it just misses a small carriage traveling on the roadway along the top of the ridge. Startled, Blackfire rears, almost falling over. Elizabeth is unseated and hits the ground.

The carriage pulls over quickly and stops. The driver jumps out and runs over to the girl. The man begins feeling the girl's head, checking for signs of blood. She starts moving, slightly. Pushing his hand away, she asks curtly, "What are you doing?" The man responds, "Are you alright? Do not move; you have had quite an upset!" Elizabeth looks at him in astonishment. Hat askew, skirt disheveled, face smudged, she says angrily, "I am fine! But you are an idiot! You could have killed me."

Surprised and vexed by her response, he looks at her now. With darkened eyes and speaking with a calm, strangely controlled voice, he responds, "I am the idiot!" He takes a small step forward, "What kind of an irresponsible person are you? You must have been riding like a banshee to come over that ridge without being able to see if anyone was on the road ahead. You should be kept at home until you know how to behave better!" He puts his hand out to help her stand up. She pushes it aside. "Look," he says, in a more conciliatory tone, "You have just had a good tumble. Let me drive you to your destination? You can tie your horse behind. I just have one stop to make." He puts his hand out; and, this time, for some reason, she takes it. She stands, shakily. Brushing off her skirt, Elizabeth walks over to her horse, which is eating grass a few feet away, and quickly moves her hand over the horse, feeling for any injuries.

She responds, "No, thank you. I have seen the way you drive a carriage. It is safer to walk!"

He says, "All right, but … ", after a furious, quelling look from Elizabeth he changes his mind, and says "If you are sure…" He nods curtly, then walks to the carriage, climbs in, and drives away, without looking back.

Elizabeth reaches to pick up the reins and notices that the horse has thrown a shoe. Wearily, she says, "Oh no!" Talking to the horse she confides, "If I did not always lose my temper so quickly, I would have had a ride home." Taking a quizzical look over her shoulder at the embankment, an expression of understanding appears upon her face. They turn in the same direction as the carriage, and slowly begin the long walk home.

In a quarter of an hour, the same carriage pulls up in front of Addington Manor; a servant comes out to take the horse's reins. The man gets out and meets Lewis at the front door. Lewis says, "His Lordship is this way." Following him, they enter the living room, where the Lord is seated comfortably.

Lewis exits, closing the door. Doctor Barnett puts his bag down near the armchair and pulls up another, smaller chair, placing it close to the Lord. He waits intently for an explanation. Without preamble or jest, Lord Addington states, "I was in the library this morning, expecting to do some paperwork; but I found I could not hold the pen and move my hand. I have been hiding that fact all day. My daughter is not home; that is why I asked you to come by. Thank you for coming." The doctor begins a careful examination.

From a distance, Elizabeth is walking her horse across a meadow and stops at a small stream, letting the horse drink the cool water. She wipes her brow with her sleeve; they both continue on.

The doctor is putting equipment back into his black bag. Solemnly, he tells the older man that he must relax. The doctor continues, "I understand you have children."

The Lord responds, "Yes. I have two. My son is a barrister with a good firm, in London. But I do not wish to bother him. He is doing well."

The doctor continues, "What about your other child?"

The Lord explains, "I have a daughter, a lovely, sweet girl. She just turned twenty years. She has been at court these last two years; but has come home to 'get a change from court life'…or so she says. But I think it was to watch over me and see that I am not doing too much. She is quite intelligent;

but I fear her feminine sensibilities would not allow for the difficult decisions and responsibilities of caring for an estate of this size."

The doctor responds, "Well, you may be right; but try to find some way to relinquish at least some of the responsibilities, so you can get some rest. I will check back with you in a few days. Before you know it, Doctor Brown will be here to take over, again."

Lord Addington says, "Thank you for coming so quickly. It was not really necessary,"

The doctor gives him a stern look, saying," Just remember what I said."

The doctor takes his bag and walks out the front door and climbs into the enclosed carriage; driving away.

Chapter 6

Just then, at the rear of the house, Elizabeth is walking her horse into the stable area. Seeing Tom, she tells him that Blackfire has thrown a shoe; they had to walk home. Tom acknowledges, takes the reins, and talking calmly to the horse, leads him into the stable.

Crossing the yard, Elizabeth enters the house, and heads upstairs to her bedroom. She calls to Fiona that she will need a bath and will be changing into something informal, just to join her father for whatever is left from lunch. Fiona notifies Lewis, then comes into her room and begins to help.

Lewis informs His Lordship that Lady Elizabeth is back from her ride and will join him for lunch. Lord Addington cautions Lewis not to tell her that the doctor was here, today!

After washing up and changing clothes, she moves slowly down to the dining room to join her father.

Almost done with his meal, he stays, to spend some time with his daughter.

Elizabeth enters happily, slightly sore from the earlier fall. She walks over to her father and kisses him quickly. She sits, and begins plating her dish.

Lord Addington comments, "You appear to be quite happy!"

Elizabeth replies, "Well… I am happy to see you!"

"And how was your morning?" He asks. "I was able to get some long-overdue correspondences done before riding. Then, Blackfire threw a shoe, and we walked back. I would have arrived even later, except that we crossed through every neighbor's property taking short cuts. So, I got my exercise by walking him back." Her father says, "Oh, my dear, I hope it was not too long of a walk!" Elizabeth, avoiding his gaze, replies, "No, we had not gone very far."

A servant enters the dining room, holding a silver tray with two letters. He leans toward Elizabeth with the tray. She reaches for both letters. She reads one out loud, saying, "John says he will be coming soon, for a visit." Opening the other letter, she tells her father, "Hugh and Letitia will be stopping by tonight, to take me to the dinner party at Lady Margaret's. They will be here at 8 PM. Oh! It also says they will be bringing another guest with them, too. I should like to meet her!"

Looking at her father, "Well, there are some things I must take care of, so I need to hurry along, now." Lord Addington says, "My dear, you should not be working so hard. There are others whom I can get to do things. Just tell me what you would like done; I will arrange it."

Elizabeth says, "I know you would, and I love you for it. But it pleases me to do something useful. I cannot explain it; but there you are! You have a daughter who can neither sing nor sew; but can plant a garden and organize…things. The dinner party at Margaret's is only a light meal, so, I will see you before I leave." Speaking earnestly to her father, she says, "Try to get some rest until then!" She gets up from the table, leaving the room.

Lord William Addington's expression turns to one of worry and discomfort.

Chapter 7

During lunch at the Grayville Estate, Lord and Lady Grayville are discussing the evening's plans. Hugh says, "So, you are having Beth and Robert in the same carriage, tonight? And they are meeting for the first time? Letty, tell me you are not matchmaking, again."

Letitia says, "Of course not. What makes you say that?" He looks at her, with the fork halfway to his mouth. Her husband says, "It is just that she is rather…opinionated, and…well, shall we say forthright!" Letitia responds, "What you really mean is that she has some well thought-out ideas of her own and is not afraid to 'mention' them." Hugh, responds, "Well, 'mention' would be one word for it. Look, I have known Elizabeth almost as long as I have known you; and, hard as it is to believe, I agree with most of her new ideas. But she is a lot to handle on a first meeting, where no one can climb out of the carriage and leave the conversation." Letitia teasingly, says, "Handle? Did I hear you actually *use* that word?" Hugh, realizing his mistake, says, "Letty, you know what I mean." Letitia smiling sweetly, says, "Yes, and you are fortunate that I do!"

Getting up from the table, he playfully, says, "I will see you later!" Exchanging quick kisses with her, he leaves.

Addington Manor

After lunch, Lord Addington is helped to a comfortable chair on the patio, to relax.

Elizabeth can be seen in the distance wearing a sunhat and gesturing to the gardeners as to where the new small trees and bushes should be planted. She helps them move some small equipment.

London, Viscount Shelbourne Townhouse

Later in the afternoon, Elizabeth's brother, the Viscount of Shelborne, is home, at his London townhouse. A courier knocks at his door with a correspondence. The Viscount's butler opens the door; accepts the letter and takes it to the Viscount, who is enjoying a brandy in his parlor. The butler knocks on parlor door. Hears, "come" and enters. He brings the letter to the Viscount and leaves the room, closing the door. John opens the letter, reads it, and places it upon the table. It is from his sister, Beth.

Addington Manor

Having finished their plantings, Elizabeth and the gardeners collect the equipment and put the tools away. The gardeners walk in one direction, while Elizabeth heads toward the main house. She enters the house, removes her boots, hat, and work gloves. She asks a kitchen staff person to relay a message stating she will have a dinner tray in her room. Her father is also having a light dinner delivered to his room. Elizabeth undresses, bathes, has dinner, and finally gets a chance to read the newspaper. Fiona comes in, ready to help her dress and arrange her hair for tonight's party.

Her father is settled in his room by the fireplace, a good book in hand, and Leo sleeping at his feet.

Beth knocks and enters the room. Father is delighted to see her dressed up; he is reminded of just how beautiful her mother was. He says, "My dear, you look wonderful! I am sure it will not be very long before you leave here to make a lovely bride."

"I am not even thinking of that for several years. And, even then, it would have to be someone very special! Until then, you are stuck with me," she says truthfully.

Her father says, "Oh, I am sure he will be. I cannot see you settling for anyone that your heart and head did not agree on. Now, go and enjoy yourself!" She kisses him, and says, "Good night, Father."

Chapter 8

In the foyer, Lewis is answering the door just as Elizabeth comes down the stairs.

Lewis announces, "Lord and Lady Bromley are here with their carriage."

She takes her shawl from Fiona and walks outside, toward the carriage.

Climbing in, she says a friendly, "Hello everyone!" And then notices who is sitting opposite her. "You!" She exclaims. She remembers that Letitia said there would be someone else joining them. Just then, Letitia says, "Lady Elizabeth Spencer, allow me to introduce Doctor Robert Barnett, our local doctor. Robert, may I introduce my best friend, Lady Elizabeth of Addington Manor." To which they both reply, sourly, "We have met before!" Unaware of the tension, Letitia says, "Well, that is nice. Then you already know something about each other. That should make everything easier tonight." Her husband has noticed the exchange and is not so sure. But he smiles for a different reason than she suspects. She smiles at him; and their mutual love is obvious to anyone who sees this.

The carriage proceeds with all realizing that the carriage is a little too quiet. Soon it pulls up to the front of Lady Margaret Smith-Lawson's home at Ableside Hall. The interior is lit with candles and music can be heard wafting into the outside air. Chatter rings through the night from all around, as guests arrive and greet each other.

A footman helps the ladies from the carriage and all four move toward the entrance. A reception line enables the hostess, Lady Smith-Lawson, to greet each one of her invited guests in person.

Beth is surprised to see that the host knows, and appears to be friends with this country doctor. Lady Letitia Bromley introduces her dearest friend, Lady Elizabeth Spencer of Addington Manor. Lady Margaret is delighted to meet her. They make their way inside, past the ballroom.

They are moving slowly when Letty sees her friends are already at the table. Letitia moves in that direction and the three follow her across the room. At the table, Letitia makes introductions, adding Lord Edmund and Lady Sarah Wilcox to the mix of friends at the table. In a moment, Hugh rises and whispers a quick message to Letty, who nods. Robert asks Elizabeth, "May I get you a drink?" She says, "Yes, thank you." He leaves, returning with punch for everyone.

By way of conversation starters, Letty mentions that Elizabeth has been at court for the last two years and returned home, only two months ago. Letty says, "I thought it was time for her to meet some of her friendly neighbors, who support people through thick and thin. So, I brought her here!" They all toast Elizabeth; immediately she understands why Letty likes these people so much. Hugh and Letty go into the ballroom. Sarah and Edmund soon follow.

Elizabeth turns to Robert at the table and asks," So, who is minding the store while the doctor is at a party?" Robert responds, "Truth is, I was not sure I should come, tonight… my patients may need me; but I cannot remember when I have spent time in the enjoyable company of others. Letty and Hugh, I am sure, were on the verge of disowning me because I was always talking about medicine. They were probably getting bored."

Robert asks Elizabeth, "And what do you do, I mean, when you are not out riding?"

She says,"I will tell you a secret. I use it as an escape, for a little time, anyway. Not too long ago, my father had a stroke. I think so, anyway, because he never really told me. I make sure someone is aware when I am out of the house." She continues, "I love being home with him. If I never go back to court, it will be fine with me." Then, putting her fingers to her lips, says, "Oh, forgive me. I do not think I am supposed to say that!"

Conspiratorially she says, "I also have more time to read, now that I am home. But that will not last. I noticed that there is much to be done in the house and the grounds." Sighing, she continues, "Well, tonight I shall enjoy myself!" He smiles, in spite of himself, and hears himself say, "Would you care to dance?" Her smile is transforming as she says, "Yes."

Another dance starts and an unknown male guest asks Lady Elizabeth to dance. Robert moves away to stand near the wall. Two female guests engage him in conversation. They seem to have met him before. When the dance ends, Robert moves toward Elizabeth and easily begins the next dance with her. While dancing he asks, "How did you and Letty become acquainted?" She responds, "We were childhood friends. She came out into society a few years before I did. She was terribly supportive when my mother died. I love her like a sister. She met Lord Grayville at court. He is a treasure! As you can see, they are perfect for each other. Goodness, this is the most I have talked liked this to anyone."

Elizabeth asks, "Are you acquainted with many people here?" Expecting him to say no, she is surprised when he says, "Actually, yes. About half of these guests, I know on a professional basis. We do no need to let others know; so, we just nod to each other, in a silent courtesy. I see some of these people several times during the season at dinners and parties; we still just nod!"

Elizabeth smiles at him. When the dance ends, she says, "Excuse me." She walks toward a young female guest, whose face brightens when she sees Elizabeth approaching. The two embrace and move to sit on chairs away from the others. Robert watches the exchange. In a supportive show, Elizabeth takes the young guest's hands in hers and allows the young lady to do most of the talking. After a few minutes, Elizabeth gives the guest a hug that carries the heavy weight of sympathy. They separate. Robert considers this small scene and ponders that he may have to re-evaluate some ideas he has harbored, perhaps prematurely. The music stops. Dinner is announced. The guests begin to move toward their tables. Robert has waited to escort her back to their table.

Chapter 9

There is much talk going on at the table as dinner commences. Lady Sarah and Lady Elizabeth compare their stories from court. Each of the women has information and advice to offer the others on gardens, staff, and home entertaining. The conversation flows effortlessly, while servants move around, quietly seeing to the guests.

The setting, for tonight's dinner and dancing was a one-of-a-kind! Lady Margaret had tables for dining setup up in the large conservatory. The music and dancing would take place in the ballroom. The immense, glass-enclosed room was filled with candlelight, flowers, and small tables, enabling friends to dine together, enjoying more of each other's company.

It is not long before Lady Margaret comes over to their table, greeting everyone. "Now," she says, "I know most of you well enough to get your truthful response. So, please tell me, how did you like the setup this evening? You know, using the conservatory instead of the formal dining room, lots of smaller tables for seating, and the music? If you like it, then I do not need to ask anyone else. I wanted to try a little creativity; but if..." her voice trails off.

All the ladies respond enthusiastically; talking over one another!

Lady Margaret's face brightens, and she brings her hands together, almost in a clap of gratitude. She says " Thank you, this means so much to me. Since you like it, I will consider it a success. I am glad you enjoyed yourselves this evening."

As Lady Margaret walks away smiling, Elizabeth is smiling with delight, also. She has the distinct feeling that tonight was an important evening for her.

Hugh Bromley rises and says, "I will see that the carriage is brought around."

During the ride back, the carriage is again quiet; but for a different reason. Everyone has much to contemplate.

Chapter 10

Grayville Manor

Later that evening at Grayville Manor, Letty and Hugh are getting ready for bed. While Letty is brushing her hair, she slowly walks over to where Hugh is removing his boots. She moves to stand in front of him and asks, "Well, how do you think it went, tonight?" Hugh, eyeing her carefully says, "I think it went very nicely. And 'Yes', you might be right. But no more matchmaking! From here on, they work things out themselves." Letty, agreeing too quickly, says, "Yes, dear." He looks at her suspiciously, raising a brow. Then he stands, reaches for her, and kisses her soundly. Arms around him, she returns the kiss!

Shelbourne House, London

Seated at the desk in the library at Shelborne House, the Viscount has just finished writing two letters. He seals them and hands them to his butler, saying, "Please see that these are sent to the country manor and Berwick Hall, London. Also, I will need a bag packed for a two night stay at Addington. I will leave this afternoon and use the coach."

His butler responds, "Yes, your Lordship."

Closing the desk drawer, he proceeds to the dining room to have breakfast. Sitting, the servant pours coffee as he begins to eat. He considers that he will see Lady Pricilla, again, though not too soon. He has little time to spend attending parties and meeting eligible young ladies. His work at the firm is getting busier. But, he has come to appreciate and value working in the legal system. He also enjoys meeting and mingling with people who have fascinating perspectives and new ideas." *And thinking of people with new ideas, he has Elizabeth's future to consider. She should be married, and soon. Now, that is going to be a very delicate operation! And with his father not feeling well…. one thing at a time! I will know more when I visit the estate and see what is going on."*

Berwick House, London

Lady Pricilla was getting ready to go out, when the butler entered with a letter on this morning's tray. It is from John. She is visibly upset to learn that he has left town for a few days, only to visit his family at their country estate. Part of her reason for going into town, today, was to have a special evening dress commissioned, with matching shoes. She wants to be prepared when Viscount John invites her to a ball. Her mother is unaware of this new, extravagant purchase. She decides to go shopping anyway. The dress will look exceptionally beautiful on her. She will have to delay delivery, though. As she is leaving her room, the old dog is lying slightly in her path. In the spirit of revenge, she kicks the dog, which is startled and whimpers softly.

Abington Manor

In the village of Addington Manor, Elizabeth has ridden into town with a large basket of food to dispense to some families in the community who are having especially hard times. She has just come from her final stop, Mrs. Rose Burn's house. This sweet woman, who is the first one to help other neighbors, has just suffered the tragedy of a stillborn birth. She has three other children, but seems too saddened to care for herself, let alone her husband and three little ones. Having heard about this from the local vicar, she had her cook make three kinds of soup, which only needed heating. She ordered extra wood to be delivered for the stove and brought some treats for the children. Mostly, Rose just cried with gratitude and for her loss, which kept her from being able to take care of her own family. Elizabeth hugs the woman for a while; then smiles at the children as she leaves the small cottage. Robert's carriage happens to be passing on the street, when he sees Elizabeth; and for a moment, he thinks he sees her crying. Tying the carriage to the post, he gets down wondering if he can help. Taking a minute to recover herself, she hears a familiar voice say, "Lady Elizabeth, may I be of help to you?" Instantly, she knows that voice, so tender now. She turns to him with eyes full of tears and slowly leans against him, perhaps hoping that his strength would transfer to her. He puts his arms around her, saying nothing. There is no need. He has seen her basket and knows where she has just been.

Elizabeth decides she will keep in touch with the vicar and make sure that Rose has help to recover.

After using his handkerchief, several times, she says she is almost herself. And, embarrassed at her display, she begins to leave. Not wanting her to ride home like this and realizing that he does not want her to leave him, just yet….or ever, he suggests they stop in a nearby coffee shop, where she can collect her strength. And, he can better understand what just happened to him.

With the coffee and sweet scone to fortify her, Elizabeth is feeling better and apologizes to him for her behavior. She is incredulous, because she sees herself as such a sensible person. As she talks, he cannot take his eyes from her, admiring both her strength and her empathy for others. Although he appears serious, he feels like his heart is smiling. He helps her into his carriage and they proceed to Addington Manor. When the carriage arrives, almost half an hour later, the footman comes out and is surprised to see Lady Elizabeth emerging. The footman unties her horse, and walks it around back, toward the stables.

Elizabeth smiles sweetly at Robert and thanks him for his help. He nods, politely, and his carriage pulls away.

Chapter 11

Inside she learns that John has arrived and he and Father are just going into the drawing room to have a drink. She gives John a "hello" and a quick kiss, promising to come back down shortly.

Settling in comfortably, the two men talk agreeably about little things, until Elizabeth comes in.

Entering, Beth kisses her father and greets her brother, again, with a great big hug. "I am so glad you were able to get away from the office for a few days. We were both thinking that you are working too hard," says Elizabeth. "You are a fine one to talk!" Her father exclaims light heartedly. "You should see her out in the garden with the gardeners, checking on the stables, going into the village to visit, and probably more than I know about. By the way, I smelled something wonderful wafting up from the kitchen, today. When I inquired, I was told the soup was being made for someone in the village. Can you imagine?" He looks, with amazement, at John. Elizabeth adds, "I told him I love doing it. Not cooking the soup exactly, just getting some soup where it needs to be." Elizabeth, looking at John states, "And, truth be told, Father does not mind my helping others one bit."

Lewis announces dinner and the small group, enjoying friendly laughter, troops together into the dining room. During dinner, her father remembers that some mail came earlier, for Beth. He tells her that it is on the foyer table. "Would you have time to go for a ride, tomorrow morning, after breakfast?" she asks her brother. "While Majesto gets plenty of exercise, you know he loves it when you ride together. It is too bad you do not have any room for him at your townhouse." She teases. He looks upward dramatically, as if seriously pondering the idea, stating, "I do not know. Perhaps I could make room for him in one of the bedrooms. I could start a new fashion!" They all laugh.

When dinner is finished, Elizabeth takes the letter up to her bedroom and finds that it is from Letty.

Letty would like them to have dinner in the city, tomorrow, and then attend an important talk at one of the fashionable London salons. Letty's carriage could pick her up at 4:00pm. It would wait in the city for them and bring them home afterwards. "*She promises it will be enjoyable; but does not say anything about the topic.*" Elizabeth comments to herself. Knowing that almost everything Letty attends is enjoyable, Elizabeth readily accepts. She writes a quick response and asks Lewis to arrange for the letter to go to Grayville Manor first thing in the morning. Also, she and Viscount John will be riding after breakfast, tomorrow.

Enjoying a brandy after dinner, John casually asks his father if Elizabeth is 'seeing anyone' or even if she is interested in anyone. He responds, "Not that she has mentioned or that I am aware of. Why?" John carefully broaches the topic of Elizabeth possibly getting married sometime before the century is over! He continues, "And, do not so much as mention that topic, or we will both be in hot water!"

His father asks, "What about you? Is there anyone you might be interested in?" John says, "Well, there might be. There is a very lovely girl, Lady Pricilla, in London. My problem is that I think she would love to live in the country; and I cannot see myself moving that far away from the firm any time soon. I have neither the time, nor the interest in balls right now." John acknowledges, sadly," I always expected William to take over as Viscount, and then become Earl. He would have done a very fine job, indeed. I studied law because I found it exciting, never thinking that one day I would be the viscount." His father, saddened by the memory of the accidental death of his first born son, becomes quiet. He does not want his son to feel burdened with responsibilities of a life that he does not desire. The two men are silent for a while. Leo comes over to lie down next to John, so he finds himself scratching the dog's ear." How old is this dog, now?" he asks.

With breakfast over, His Lordship watches out the front window as Elizabeth and John mount their horses and head toward the village. He thinks to himself how grateful he is for all that life has given him; but he is getting tired." *It is time for someone else to take over. But, who?"*

Chapter 12

John and Elizabeth walk their horses through town. John is pleasantly surprised to see how much the town has grown. "Merchant shops, goods, services, and even street fairs, now and again! And our little church is growing, as well!" Elizabeth exclaims. "What denomination is it?" John asks. "I am not sure it is any one particular kind. Everyone is welcome and unlike many towns, no one asks. Everyone just pitches in and helps when needed. In part, no doubt, because each person knows that the day may come when they shall need help." Elizabeth says. "I think that I like that kind best of all!" John adds. Elizabeth turns to John and says, "I have a vacant shop that I would like you to see. I have an idea." John rolls his eyes and smiles at his sister.

"It is this way, only a few blocks away. Here it is." She says. "But it is empty! Are you going to fill it with your sewing and embroidery?" he teases. "Certainly not *my* embroidery!", she says, a bit exasperated. "It would be a free store to exchange items. No one would 'rent' it, but people in the community could bring in items that they no longer want or need, sell or exchange them for something they do need. No money involved! The church… I have not talked to the vicar, yet, but I am sure he would not mind helping the store open up, perhaps once each week. What do you think?" She looks at him expectantly.

"I think it is a wonderful idea. Maybe float the idea around and let the townsfolk think it is their idea. Then there could be a planning committee; you can be chairman of the board, especially since you will be 'renting' them one of the manor's buildings." John is secretly proud of his sister. Laughingly he states, "Then, when we are looking for a titled match for you, we can always say that you have experience in running a store. That should help you find a good husband." Remounting their horses, they head toward the open road and home.

Elizabeth is not deterred. She will get the name of a printer who can make some posters.

Hurrying to the dining room for lunch, she finds John and her father already there. Sitting down, she reminds them that Letitia will arrive at 4:00 PM and they are going into the city to one of the larger salons to hear a presentation. When John asks, "What is the topic?" Elizabeth responds, "I am not sure. She was rather vague on that point. It does not matter. Letitia is always willing to share her new ideas." Elizabeth does not notice her father and brother share unsettling glances.

True to her word, the coach arrives to pick up Elizabeth promptly at 4:00 PM. She is wearing one of her newest dresses and is excited about the evening's event. The ladies greet each other. Letitia explains that the guest speaker is someone very special, known to many Londoners because of her exquisite letter writing. She explains, "This event is by invitation, only. Otherwise, there would be too many people coming for the size of the salon." As they arrive, Letty tells

Elizabeth to stay near her. "At events this important, the men sometimes forget their manners and begin pushing ladies aside to get closer to the speaker. When the presentation is over, that is when it becomes a madhouse. Everyone gets up and starts moving together. It gets a little crushing and you can get lost in the crowd." Elizabeth understands. It will start in about ten minutes, so they move toward their reserved seating. As the gong is sounded, people move quickly to their seats and quiet descends on the room.

Chapter 13

Entering the raised platform from a side entrance is Dr. Robert Barnett. Elizabeth is startled to see him, let alone up on the stage. Opening the remarks, he thanks everyone for coming and promises them an enlightening evening, full of new ideas. He begins to present some background information on the special guest speaker.

"The person you shall hear will be speaking about true, personal experiences of travels, people, culture, and medicine. Yes, things that have been experienced firsthand.

"You see, our guest has been in Turkey, spending two years in the Ottoman Empire. Letters she has written to friends, here in England, express in finest literary detail, the secular world of the Muslim Orient.

"More than that though, she brought back a life-saving gift for all of us. You are aware that England, and other countries, suffered enormously from the epidemic disease called smallpox. While she was living in Turkey, our guest witnessed how the Turks treated this disease and have all but gotten rid of this most painful, degrading, and deadly disease. Would we not want the same for our loved ones… our country? I have the pleasure of introducing to you the person who introduced smallpox inoculation to England, saving countless lives. Friends, I give you, Lady Mary Wortley-Montagu!" The audience breaks into a thunderous applause. Elizabeth surveys the audience and sees expressions of recognition and pleasure on so many faces.

After a moment, Lady Wortley-Montagu is seated in a comfortable chair and she starts her address. She explains how her brother died from smallpox and that she did not fully escape its disfiguring marks. She recounts how, in 1717, having traveled with her husband to his Ambassador assignment in Constantinople, she witnessed the 'inoculation' procedure; and how thousands of Turks line up each year to have a small amount of the pus from a pox scraped into the arm or leg. This small amount, called 'engrafting,' promotes immunity. Although the person will experience some very light symptoms, they will not experience the pain, disfigurement, and sometimes death, which we have seen in epidemics. When, in 1721, that epidemic hit England, she had her own daughter inoculated. Many people risked the inoculation, while others wanted nothing to do with it. Those are the ones who died. She said Princess Caroline, after testing the treatment on seven prisoners, all of whom lived after being inoculated, decided to have both of her daughters inoculated against smallpox. She went on to encourage everyone to challenge some long-held ideas and cultural norms that hinder scientific advancement, moral lives, and intellectual growth. After listening to her speak for almost two hours, and answering questions, Elizabeth was mesmerized by this most unusual woman, Lady Mary Wortley-Montagu. She was not sure she had even taken a breath, until the woman finished. Elizabeth realized that something inside her had changed; that she would never be quite the same. She made a mental note to add *Letters from Turkey* to her reading list. As Letty predicted, once the presentation ended, the crowd surged together. And, not being as tall as the men, ladies lost sight of each other. Robert remained on stage a little while longer, personally thanking Lady Mary and others who had helped organize the event. By the time he could get away, he had lost sight of Letty and Elizabeth. Letty thought it might have been a good idea if she and Elizabeth had worn colorful hats so they could be seen. Unable to move away from the crowd, Elizabeth was pushed along, toward the doors. Taking a chance, she pushed herself toward the wall, so the crowd went around her. Searching frantically from his elevated place on the stage, Robert scans the room and seeing Letty, calls loudly, trying to get her attention. The crowd near her had dissipated so she could stand still, and just wait for him to come over. Now, both of them looked about for Elizabeth. Then, they heard a voice, clearly raised, saying, "Stop pushing me, you oaf!" And they would know that voice anywhere. Holding tight to Letty's hand Robert fairly pulled her toward the wall and found their friend, only slightly less the worse for wear. Waiting until most of the group had exited the salon, they finally went outside. Straightening her hat, Elizabeth calmly states, "Well, that was exciting!" "Which part?" asks Robert. Elizabeth emphatically says, "All of it! We should do this more often." Robert and Letty look at her; she in disbelief, and he with renewed appreciation. Robert offers to take them for a light supper; but Letty demurs, saying it would be late enough, by the time they got home. Hiding her disappointment, Elizabeth walked with the two toward Letty's coach. As the driver got down to assist them, Letty and Elizabeth thanked him for the invitations and the extraordinary evening. As they pulled away, Robert stood there, watching the coach until it was too dark to be seen.

On the way home, Letty asks Elizabeth if she would like to meet for tea, tomorrow. Elizabeth agrees, if they can meet just a little later in the morning. She says she will probably sleep in for a few minutes more. Letty agreed, thinking she could use a little respite from tonight's excitement, as well.

Chapter 14

By the time the coach reached Elizabeth's house, dinner was long finished. John and his father were ensconced in the drawing room; John was reading and His Lordship, with his eyes closed, was 'thinking.' The men, startled by Leo's reaction to the coach pulling up, knew that Elizabeth was home. Removing her somewhat crushed hat and cloak, she headed right for the drawing room.

Lewis asks, "Have you had dinner, my Lady?" "No, I have not." She responds. "Would it be too much to have a tray of something sent to my room? I am famished and tired," she admits.

"I will see to it right away," Lewis said.

Entering the room, she began telling them about her evening with Letty and Robert. She did not stop until she explained the pushing and impolite men at the end. Clearly, she had been enthralled. John calmly asked, "Who is Robert?" Elizabeth replied, "He is dad's doctor! Letty got the invitations to the event from him." Keeping his thoughts to himself, John does not tell Elizabeth that 'the doctor' was coming tomorrow morning. He would have a talk with this man.

Attesting to her appearance, Elizabeth said she was tired and was going to her room. Saying 'good night' to them both, she heads for the stairs. John and his father looked at each other with curious expressions." I think I will head up, now, too. See you at breakfast, John." "Good Night, Dad," John stays in the room, thinking, for almost another hour.

In another part of town, Doctor Robert Barnett was excited about the evening, too. Lady Mary had been every bit the success he thought she would be. She was the daughter of the third Earl of Denbigh. An aristocrat, she was known to London society as beautiful, charming, and the toast of the season, before smallpox. But, hearing her speak would get more people to learn about the procedure of inoculation, and understand that smallpox does not have to be the death sentence it has been. And then, he thought of Elizabeth! *It was heartwarming to see that she would be interested in a presentation such as this. Most ladies would not even consider attending. But there she was. What was that feeling that had come over him so thoroughly when she had been lost to him, in the crowd. Fear?Anger? Not to see her ever again was unthinkable. It was at that moment he knew he loved her.*

With thoughts of Elizabeth, he finally fell asleep. He had been in bed for less than an hour when his doorbell rang. Someone needed him and apparently, it could not wait. He got ready to go.

Chapter 15

Following the rider, Robert arrived at a small cottage just outside of town. The door was flung open as soon as he dismounted. A young girl led him to the bedroom where her mother was in the throes of childbirth. A midwife, who had been present from the beginning of labor, sent for him because she could tell that the baby had not turned in the womb and was still in a breach position. In an attempt to give the family members something to do with themselves, he asked for soap, hot water, and clean linens. Removing his coat and rolling up his sleeves, he went to the young woman, took her hand in his and told her who he was. Speaking calmly, he asked her to help him deliver this baby, safely, by doing exactly as she was told. Would she do this? The woman nodded 'Yes' He then told the family, which consisted of her husband and a seven year old daughter, that they could stay if they could be quiet and also did what they were told. Both of them tired, afraid, and wanting to do something said "yes" eagerly. With the soap he washed his hands thoroughly. He told the girl to keep wiping her mother's brow. He told the father it would be a big help if he held his wife's hand and spoke words of encouragement. And so it began. After both he and the midwife washed their hands, he explained that he was going to try to turn the baby's position, so that the head would deliver first. This would be uncomfortable, but he would do it slowly. Looking meaningfully at the husband for a moment, they both understood that this part was critical.

Robert told them, "Sometimes a baby will turn on its own, at the last minute. We just need to give it a little help to go in the right direction." Applying pressure to the stomach area, he felt the baby move slightly in the womb. Doing this slowly and gently, several more times over a period of an hour, the baby was finally in position.

The mother was exhausted; but doing well, with her supporters, on each side. Robert could now see the head was beginning to crown. With that, the mother screamed and made an involuntary push. Guiding her, she pushed a few more times and the baby came out quickly, wailing loudly. Everyone's faces, all at the same time, changed to relief and joy. Robert cleaned the infant, wrapped it in clean linen, and handed it to the midwife, who got the pleasure of announcing, "You have a son!", as mother and father began to cry tears of joy, Robert finished ministering to the mother, confirming that the bleeding was slowing. Taking a minute, he purposely looked at the little girl, solemnly telling her, "You did an excellent job helping your mother. You have no idea how important it is for the mother to have her brow wiped. Thank you for your help." The girl's face literally beamed. He continued, "Your mother may need some more help over the next few days; I am hoping that you, as the big girl now, can do this for her." The girl's head nodded vigorously in assent. While the bed linens were changed, Robert moved away to scrub his hands and arms. After pulling down his sleeves, he put his coat on.

Before leaving, Robert spoke to the older midwife quietly, "Thank you for your assistance. The mother and baby could have died if you had not called me." She told him, "I was hoping you were not one of those doctors who show up with dirty hands, never washing them. Because, I have seen too many women sick, after giving birth like that. I cannot explain it: but, some things, you just know." He asked for her name and where she lived. He added, "Would you want to assist me, again, if needed?" She said, "I would be very pleased to help and to learn as much as I could." She confided to Robert that her only daughter had died giving birth, while she was away. She never wanted that to happen to any other woman.

After checking on the mother and telling her he would visit in two days, he left.

Body tired, but mind fully awake, he wondered why giving birth, even in a hospital, nowadays, had become so dangerous for mothers. He, too, knew of women, in lying-in hospitals, who were healthy throughout the pregnancy, but died a few days later. He vowed to contact some of his research friends and find out more about this.

Chapter 16

It was almost 5:00 AM when he arrived home. After a quick wash up, he slid into bed and was asleep with minutes. Having slept deeply for two hours, he arose washed, dressed, and had a small breakfast. He had an appointment, of sorts, at the home of a young boy from the village, who had fallen out of a tree and broken his arm. After checking the bandage and splint, looking for any unusual swelling or discoloration, and checking for overheating, he told the parents that the break was healing nicely—but to limit the boy's activities. Otherwise, the break may not heal properly. The grateful mother offered him some coffee, but he declined, saying he had another patient to visit. This was partly true. The carriage drove away, heading for Addington Manor.

Leaving the Manor, at that very moment was Elizabeth, on her way to meet Letty for breakfast in the village. Waiting for their food to be prepared Letty said,"I have noticed that some people are starting to drink tea, instead of coffee. Can that be right?" Elizabeth said, "I have read in the newspaper that England is now getting tea supplied all the way from the West Indies. It seems ships are carrying more and more of it because it is in great demand." Letty replied, "Well I cannot see anyone liking tea more than coffee! I am certainly in favor of one product that is coming to England, sugar! Shops have the most delightful treats, and our cook is going to try to get some recipes." The subject turned to the evening with Mary Wortley-Montagu. "I will tell you,

Letty, I thought she was extraordinary. I would love to hear more presentations like that," Elizabeth stated confidently. As the breakfast arrived, she continued, "But, I could not understand why Robert was there? He seemed to command a certain respect. I am surprised he figured so prominently in the event!" Letty looked slightly confused, for the moment. Then recognition set in and she said," I understand, now. I am so sorry; I thought you knew." A little exasperated, but still eating, Elizabeth said, "Know what? I know he is a country doctor!" "But that is just it. He is *not* just a country doctor," Letty corrected and went on. "He does not like to mention his title and his good friends certainly do not bring it up. But he is actually the Earl of Westerbrook. He simply loves being a doctor and he is very good at it, I must say." As Letty finished explaining, the look on Elizabeth's face made her burst into laughter.

When Robert's carriage arrives at Addington Manor, the footman opened the door; but it was the Lordship's son, Viscount Shelbourne, who was waiting inside for him. Introducing himself to the doctor, the Viscount asks if he might speak with him in the library, after he had seen his father. "Certainly," Robert responded.

Spending some time with His Lordship, he found him, as he explained, "… to be having increased difficulty moving about, as he once did." His Lordship also confessed that he had some memory loss, as well. And, he was keeping this information from his children." He surmised, to Robert,

"The real reason John has come was to check up on him. No doubt initiated by the concerns from Elizabeth. I have noticed that worried look on her face, even though she tries to hide it. I do not want to feel that I cannot be truthful with them; but I think they may reorder their lives because of this. And I do not want them to do that!" he states emphatically. Robert says to him, "We have been honest with each other and I appreciate your trust in me. My advice is to take each day as it comes and do the best you can." Continuing, Robert says, "I will share as much or as little as you want. I think it is best if you, on your own terms, explain the truth of your condition. It may give them some courage, in the future, when they need it." Nodding slowly, His Lordship says, "You are right. I will talk to John and Elizabeth this afternoon. Thank you, again, for your service, and may I say 'friendship' also." Robert leaves the room quietly, while the older man rests and thinks.

Chapter 17

Hearing him come down the stairs, John stepped out of the library and motioned for Robert to join him. "Please, come in and sit. How is your day going? "John asked, by way of small talk. In response, Robert says, "Well, considering I returned home about 5:00 AM after delivering a baby, got two hours rest, then checked on a young boy with a broken arm, it has been pretty busy." Just then Lewis knocked and opened the door, bringing in a tray of scones and hot coffee. Robert could not keep his face from smiling with delight. "I always like a cup, halfway through the morning," John lies.

While Robert enjoyed the coffee, John carefully broached his topic.

"Elizabeth told us about the wonderful presentation she and Letty went to hear, in London. I must say that it is probably not somewhere I would have taken a young lady, but my sister is, well, let us say, not cut from the same cloth as some other ladies. And, while I love her being curious about new ideas and compassionate toward others, I also worry about her. She will have to marry in another year or so. When I become the Earl, I will see to it that she is taken care of, naturally." John asks, "Now, I would like to know something about you; since you have been caring for my father and he seems to have faith in you, which is hard for him to come by."

Robert gives him the broader strokes, "I graduated from Oxford and spent a few years studying with some preeminent professors and physicians. Right now, I am covering for Doctor Brown, who will be back from Northumberland after spending time with family. I see many changes coming in the field of medicine, and I am not exactly sure where I want to concentrate. I just know that I love what I am doing."

"Where are you living?" John continues. "I have a small flat outside London, which allows me to move between city and country estates. So it is ideal." "Is that it?" John asks surprised and maybe a little disappointed. "No, there is my estate in Essex. I am actually the Earl of Westerbrook. I do not use my title. I find it gets in the way of what I like to do, more than it helps with anything. I will confide something to you. My younger brother and I have an arrangement. I love being a doctor and he loves running the estate. I might say he is very good at it. I rarely question anything he does. He lives there with his wife of over a year. She is pregnant now. I love them dearly! Is there anything else?" Robert questions, nicely.

Having been broadsided by this excellent news, John, smiling, says, "There is just one more thing. If your schedule permits, would you be able to join us for dinner, tomorrow night?"

Robert smiles, stands and says, "I would be delighted to join you. I thank you for the excellent coffee and conversation. As for your father, he will want to talk to you and Elizabeth, today. Now, I must see about my next patient. Good day, and thank you, again. I shall see you tomorrow." Robert stands, retrieving his bag.

John is delighted. Perhaps a plan can be devised. He also realizes that during his stay, he has only thought of Pricilla once. *I should send her a letter. Maybe not!*

Chapter 18

Just before lunch, John asks to see Elizabeth in the library, before their father wakes from his nap.

"How was your outing with Letty, today?" John inquires. "It was nice," She says brusquely. "But, do you know what I found out? It seems that the doctor, who has been seeing Father, is not really a country doctor, at all!" Elizabeth announces. "Oh, my goodness, do not tell me he is a barber or one of those fellows who pretends to know something about medicine," John dramatizes.

"Well, no, of course not." Elizabeth answers, perplexed. "Then, he is a doctor?" John continues the ruse. "Yes, of course he is a doctor. Do you think I would let just anybody take care of our father?" "Then what is the problem?" John asks. "He... he, did not portray himself in a truthful manner!" Elizabeth blurts out. "Oh, I see. Perhaps if he had told you that he was an Earl, you might have treated him a little nicer? Been more polite, more ladylike? " John supposes. "No, I would most likely have been myself." She admits, as John winces. Continuing, Elizabeth describes their encounter. "I think, we got off on the wrong foot, at the very beginning. But I must confess that he has always acted the gentleman toward me. When we were together, with friends, at Lady Margaret's party, I realized that I had not the full measure of the man. There may actually be much to commend him." She states, reluctantly.

"High praise indeed! So you do not hate the man?" John pushes. "No, probably not." she says weakly. "Well, it is good to know that you are not too vexed with him, because I invited him to dinner, tomorrow night."

London, Berwick House

At the Berwick House, London, events have cast a somber mood over all. Lady Margery's lovable dog and companion, Barry, has become seriously ill, for no apparent reason. The young girl will not be moved from the dog's side. Pricilla has received a letter from John, saying that his return will be delayed another two days, and Lord Berwick has suffered a setback in his financial affairs.

ADDINGTON MANOR

The morning paper is once again on the table. Elizabeth reads aloud an article about a fire in another town, across the county. She is surprised to learn of the loss of life and property because there was no organized approach for the community to get it under control, quickly. Elizabeth comments, "How very sad, and awful! We should look into this. Well, I will, anyway."

Over breakfast, all three discuss their plans for the day. At his father's request, John will ride into London and visit a lawyer-friend and have him look over his father's will. He will be back before their dinner, tonight. Elizabeth asks if she might go to London with him, as there is a print shop she needs to visit. "Well, that leaves me to mind the store," His

Lordship teases. "Go about your business, we will meet for drinks before our friend arrives."

Elizabeth gives him a questioning look at the term 'friend' that he has just used. But, she says nothing.

Later that morning, on their way to London, John asks Elizabeth, "Would you mind if we stopped, for a brief visit, at a friend's house?" I can send a messenger to her house, letting her know we are coming?" With a wry smile, Elizabeth asks, "And, is this lady someone special?" John responds, "In truth, I am not sure, yet. But I would like you to meet her."

While John spends time in the lawyer's office, Elizabeth has located the print shop and is wondering about the crowd that has gathered outside the store. Everyone seems to be staring at something in the window. As she gets closer, she realizes a copy of today's newspaper, printed by the shop, has been hung up in the window, for all to see. Entering the store, she shows a young clerk named Ben, a copy of a poster and a flyer that she wants printed.

The flyer needs about fifty copies made, because they will be handed out to the community, she explains. Deciding on wording and type size, she is happy with the information and advice she receives from him. Before she leaves, she says, "Your accent tells me you are not from London. Did you just move here?" he replies, pleasantly, "No, my Lady. I am here from the colonies."

As John enters the store, she turns to thank the young man for his help. Walking to a small food shop they observe that London seems more crowded than ever; and it appears to grow more crowded every month. After having a light meal, they take the carriage to Berwick House.

Chapter 19

Upon entering the house, they realize that all is not well. Margery is crying, inconsolably, Pricilla is annoyed with her sister's display, and the parents, although courteous enough, are stressed.

Pricilla guides the pair to the drawing room. While she is very happy to see John, Elizabeth gets the impression that it does not follow that Pricilla wanted to see Elizabeth. She sends for tea.

John asks Pricilla, "What has happened with Margery? She sounds distraught." Pricilla explains, "Oh, it is really nothing. Her dog was sick a few days and he died this morning. She is just making a big event out of it. This is why I will never have a dog in my house. They get in the way, and then they die!" John's face has an expression that Elizabeth cannot read because she has never seen it before. Elizabeth excuses herself and leaves the room. She finds Margery sitting on the stairs, her head leaning on the railing. Elizabeth climbs the few stairs and sits next to the girl. She say,"I am so sorry to hear about your dog. I have a dog, too. Well, he really belongs to all of us. But I would feel just as you do if anything happened to him." To her surprise, the girl slowly turns and put she tear-stained face against Elizabeth's shoulder. Elizabeth finds herself patting the girl's back and being sorrowful, too. Handing the girl a handkerchief from her own pocket, she asks the girl to join her in the drawing room for tea. "Tea always helps to make things a little better." Elizabeth smiles and with her new 'friend' holding her hand, enters the room. Pricilla's polite expression disappears for an instant, then reappears; but Elizabeth has seen it pass, and she knows what it means. Pricilla has a jealous nature! She asks her younger sister, "Do you not have something to do?" Elizabeth states, "I asked her to join us. She seemed miserable." "Oh, that dog, again." Pricilla rolls her eyes. John and Elizabeth do not stay long after finishing the tea.

After picking up her printed materials, Elizabeth and John head home.

Sadly, John remarks, "I am glad you came with me, today. You are a kind person!" Elizabeth is silent.

At home, Elizabeth looks again at her poster and flyers. Tomorrow, she will meet the carpenter, who is going to fix a few things in the community building. Elizabeth will put the poster up in the front window. There will be another item on the meeting agenda: starting a town fire brigade! They will need a committee. She will find out what other towns are doing.

A few things to do and then she must get ready for the dinner. For reasons she has not taken time to consider, she wants to look especially nice. Shortly before dinner, she meets her two favorite gentlemen in the living room. As Elizabeth enters, they are pleasantly surprised to see her wearing a new outfit, looking radiant. Taking a glass of wine from John, she smiles.

In a few minutes, Lewis announces, "the Earl of Westerbrook," and Robert enters.

He, too, has taken special care with his suit. Greeting His Lordship and the Viscount, he turns to Elizabeth and the look he bestows on her says only one thing! Elizabeth accepts his outstretched hand graciously, while smiling broadly at his expression.

During dinner, the foursome exchange ideas and news about the government, medicine, and the local village. Since each of them interacts with a different portion of society, the conversation is both enlightening and enjoyable. After dinner and dessert, His Lordship makes his excuse, saying, "My doctor tells me to get more rest, so this once I am going to take his advice." Looking at Robert, he thanks him sincerely. Kissing his daughter and waving to John, His Lordship leaves the room. With his valet ready to assist him, they mount the stairs.

John confides to Elizabeth and Robert that he has decided to set up a new law office closer to the manor and London. He will still keep the townhouse, using it for important events in London. He will also continue to work with his large law firm, when needed. Although, he sees his work divided between the practice of law and overseeing the estate. John explains to Robert that they had an older brother who was to naturally inherit the title, but died in a tragic accident and this was how John became the Viscount.

"And I, of course, having no title, profession, or higher education am kept in abeyance until the moment I am told what to do!" Elizabeth protests. "My dear sister," John states, "in your whole life, I have never seen you in 'abeyance'. You are always busy! And, as for being told what to do, well, Robert and I know how well that works!" Robert judiciously remains quiet on that subject; but he cannot keep himself from smiling. Here is a family that loves each member, just as his own does. He savors the thought. After a while, the evening is over. After thanking his host and hostess, Robert leaves. John checks on a few things; Elizabeth, exhausted, goes up to bed.

Chapter 20

After breakfast, John prepares to return to London and the office.

His father is feeling especially cheery. Later in the morning, Elizabeth goes into town and meets the carpenter at the community building. She has ideas about adding more windows to let in the light and fresh air. Then, she will see Mrs. Burn, hoping that she is feeling better. She plans on asking if the family wants for anything. Robert has been to visit the woman who delivered the baby boy and to check on the arm of the boy who fell out of the tree.

As they are making their rounds in town, Robert and Elizabeth happen to see each other. He crosses the street to come over to talk to her. She smiles broadly upon noticing him. He asks if she has time, would she like to try some tea, in about an hour. He has one more stop to make. She tells him she will be at the dressmakers, across the street and to come there when ready. He agrees. *Going to a dressmaker!* He thinks to himself, *That has to be a first and maybe, if he is lucky, it will not be the last.* After a minute, he concedes, *I would go anywhere with her,* and smiles.

While having their tea, which they both agreed to try, Robert says, "If I recall correctly, there may have been only two instances when we have been alone, and one of those times you were yelling at me." Elizabeth opens her mouth to defend herself; Robert raises his finger, wanting to continue,

"I would like to see you more often, if it does not involve any raised voices. Would that be something you would like to try? If not, if I have misjudged anything, please let me know." Robert's expression is one of hope, and possible resignation. It does not take long for Elizabeth to give her answer. "I think that would be most enjoyable; if you agree not to yell at me, either." Robert suggests, "Let us both agree to work on that very hard! Doctor Brown will be back in two weeks to resume his practice. After that, I have committed to another medical presentation, in London. It is still in the planning stage. However, I would like to stop at your house, tomorrow morning, for a brief visit. If you still feel the same, perhaps we could go for a ride in the country, in a carriage. Will you be available after breakfast?" "Yes, that would be fine. Should I drive the carriage, or you?" she asks, with feigned sweetness and docility. Robert sees that look and bursts out laughing. "Shall we go?" he asks. Both standing, he moves his hand protectively to her back.

In the ensuing weeks, Lady Elizabeth and Lord Westerbrook are seen together during the season's social life of dinners and balls, walking and riding in town, and enjoying conversations with Lord William and Viscount John. Until one Saturday afternoon in early May, the Earl of Westerbrook sends a message to Lord William, asking to meet with him if he has time. It is then, dressed in his finest suit, that the Earl of Westerbrook asks for Lady Elizabeth's hand in marriage. Pretending to keep Robert waiting while he decides, Lord William affects a very serious expression, then with a bright smile and a hand outstretched exclaims, "I am pleased beyond all measure, my good fellow!" He continues, "I could not see her with anyone else. You are both well-matched; I think you will be very happy, together. Have you spoken to Elizabeth?"

Westerbrook responds, "No, I thought I would ask her tonight, just before we have dinner."

"Excellent! Then let us have a toast to our good fortune: I will not have her telling me what I can and cannot do, now you will have to hear her tell *you* what you can and cannot do," Lord William laughs, good naturedly. "I must be off, now. Not a word! I shall see you and John, tonight," Robert establishes.

As Elizabeth comes downstairs that evening, she learns that her father and brother are taking an especially long time getting ready for dinner. Just then the front door is opened. Robert enters, looking handsome as ever. Lord Addington has given Lewis strict orders not to allow anyone to enter the living room, until he comes down. Alone with Elizabeth, Robert stands in front of her, gently taking her hands in his. Looking into her questioning eyes, he says, "Elizabeth, I have found my life's joy in spending time with you. From now on, I would like us to walk through life together, sharing the good times and bad. I love you! And if you love me too, please, say that you will marry me. Will you marry me?" The look on her face was one he was not expecting. With difficulty, Elizabeth says, "Robert, I love you. I will always love you, but

I cannot marry you!" Stricken, he asks simply, but strongly, "Why?" Her eyes well up with tears, "I cannot tell you the reason." He looks at her completely dumbfounded and now chagrined. Hearing the knock on the door, he sees William and John enter, talking jovially. Elizabeth bursts into tears and hurries from the room. Robert says, "Excuse me." and leaves the room quickly, asking for his cloak. John turns to his father and asks, "Does this mean there will only be two of us for dinner?" Elizabeth can be heard weeping in her room, but the door is locked, and no one knows what has happened. Robert spends the night at his flat in London because that is closer than driving to the estate in Essex and because he fears, in his condition, he may run the carriage off the road.

He will give her some time; she may tell him what on earth is on her mind.

Having felt such joy thinking that she may be his, only to have his spirit dashed, knowing that it will not happen, has left him bereft!

Chapter 21

Over the next few weeks, they both take the same approach toward putting the 'situation' behind them. They throw themselves into their work. Robert works hard on a medical paper and is spending time at Oxford with fellow physicians.

Elizabeth makes little time for friends or talking. She continues to work with Wrede and is now making most of estate decisions. Her community trading hall is a success, with villagers trading time, talent, and household items. A pleasant side effect is that more villagers know each other and are willing to help their neighbors. She has also purchased a list of items needed for the fire brigade. Most for the merchants have agreed to be part of the brigade because they know how dangerous it is for a fire to start anywhere in town. Groups of men will learn how to operate the pump and hoses. Elizabeth thinks, *Maybe they should have a practice, too.*

Lord William has changed, too. He is quiet and has lost his energy and appetite. John is completely perplexed about the whole situation. So, he keeps himself busy and out of the way.

One day, when Robert is in town he hears an unfamiliar bell ringing, then dozens of men drop what they are doing and immediately run to different positions, all performing coordinated actions, of some type. He watches with interest. A pail, filled with hay, has been carefully set on fire. One person appears in the road and is shouting to the men with the water buggy. Two men take their places and start furiously pumping. The fire is quickly doused; the practice is considered a success. Coming around the corner, holding the still-smoking pail is Elizabeth. Robert see her and smiles, "I should have known!" He moves back, before she sees him; and turns to go the other way.

The next day Elizabeth receives a letter from Letitia. She and Hugh have been away for three weeks, at Letty's sister's house because she was having a baby. Letty tells Elizabeth that her sister had a beautiful baby girl two weeks ago. Having spent time with her sister to help out with the baby, she and Hugh are now at home. Letty would like Elizabeth to come to her house for coffee. Would Elizabeth be available to come in two days, on Thursday afternoon? Elizabeth responds she would love to have coffee with her on Thursday.

The following day, Elizabeth is in town, having a committee meeting with the Community Market Group, as it is now called. The official opening will be in three weeks. A few special events are being planned for that day, to attract people from other towns. It was decided that Elizabeth would write a small article for the area newspaper to draw attention to the event.

At the same time, Robert was not far away meeting with Doctor Brown, who returned a few days prior. Robert was explaining the patients' care and progress of the cases.

Everyone's normal routine was interrupted, one day, when the fire bell started ringing and did not stop.

Rushing outside, she saw that the blacksmith's shop, located a few doors down, across the street, had flames quickly growing inside. As usual, the front doors were wide open. Seeing the men were helping the blacksmith out of the building, all Elizabeth could think of was, "There must be a horse still inside!" The horse was neighing wildly, the fire brigade hooking up hoses, and people congregating in the street added to the confusion. Frantic to do something, Elizabeth doused herself with water and covered her mouth with a wet handkerchief. She raced toward the barn and hurried inside. Blinded by the smoke, she followed the sound of the horse. Opening his stall door to pull him out, the horse only backed up, resisting her attempts to help him leave his stall. Beginning to breathe deeply, because of the struggle, Elizabeth began to cough from the lack of air. Robert was down the street and recognized that colorful skirt just as it disappeared inside the barn. Covering his head with his jacket, Robert ran in after her. Hearing her cough, he made his way toward the sound. Seeing her struggle, he took the horse's reins from her hand, and caught her, just as she collapsed. Heading toward the noise from outside, they reached doorway just as a beam fell down behind them. With Doctor Brown attending the blacksmith, Robert carried an unconscious Elizabeth across the street, into the community building. He asked a youth to quickly bring his bag from the carriage outside and a small pail of water. Wiping her face and assuring himself she was breathing, he opened his bag and got out smelling salts. Slowly coming around, she opened her eyes, and starting coughing…and coughing! "You have some smoke in your lungs. Do not move. Just take small breaths, quietly. Keep the cool, wet, cloth over your eyes and mouth," He said, trying to keep the anger out of his voice, thinking, *"No sense in scaring the patient, right now. That will come later."* Putting his jacket under her head, he told her, "Do not move an inch or so help me…. I am going outside to check if there are any other injuries." When he found Doctor Brown, he was tending to several burns on the blacksmith; none of them life threatening. He explained to the doctor there had been only one horse inside the barn and that he was in the Community Market building tending to Elizabeth, who had suffered smoke inhalation. The fire brigade's quick and efficient response was able to save most of the building. Robert told Doctor Brown, "I am going to drive Elizabeth home, where she can relax and recuperate. Should you need me, send word to Addington Manor." Returning to Elizabeth, he asked her, in a softer tone, "How do you feel? A little better?" She nodded, unable to speak. The boy looks on wide-eyed. Robert, smiling, takes a silver coin from his pocket and gives it to the boy, "Thank you, for your help." Scooping up Elizabeth, he puts her in his carriage and driving slowly to minimize her coughing, takes her home.

Chapter 22

The footman came out to the carriage, immediately. Robert carried her inside and is shown where her room is located. He asked Fiona, "Could you please make some tea with honey, not hot, just barely warm"

Lord William, hearing all the commotion, hurries into her room. Robert explains to him, "There was a fire at the blacksmith's in town. In her haste to help, Elizabeth went inside the barn to save a horse." Elizabeth, unable to speak, gives Robert such an acrimonious expression that he should have cared. But he did not. She was safe and that was all that mattered to him. "Here, take this with your tea," he says to Elizabeth. Speaking to her father, he says, "I have given her something to help her sleep, tonight. It will also help her throat. She got smoke in it. So, she is to do no talking, just yet." Sighing, he said, "I will have Doctor Brown stop in tomorrow to check on her." Surprised, Lord William said, "But, can *you* not come?" Robert responded, "She is not my patient, anymore; she is Doctor Brown's. I will see myself out."

In the morning, Elizabeth still resting in bed, sends off a message to Letty telling her she cannot meet her for coffee; she had a slight accident. Letty sends a message back, telling her she will come to the manor to see her.

Letty has read the local newspaper and knows about the fire. She learns that the fire brigade did an excellent job putting out the fire and Lady Elizabeth, of Addington Manor, went into the burning barn and saved a horse.

She is both surprised and impressed; even more eager to hear what Elizabeth has to say!

Disappointed and feeling sorry that Elizabeth cannot talk without coughing, Letty stops questioning her. Instead, Letty tells her about the visit to her sister's house. She decides to ask Robert over for dinner, sure that plans have been moving toward their engagement. Letty will catch up on all the news with Elizabeth when she feels better.

That evening, at dinner with Letty and Hugh, the whole story comes out: Robert asking Elizabeth to marry him, Elizabeth saying 'no', and not telling him why. After that, it seemed that both he and Elizabeth became very busy, avoiding each other. He confesses he was miserable, and it took all his strength not to go see her. "Since Elizabeth told me she loves me, how could this be? She loves me; but, she refuses to marry me!" Robert says, astounded.

Letty, is quiet for a moment; then, with a simple air of understanding and command of the situation, she states, "I know why!" Robert and Hugh look at her, clearly waiting for an explanation. Letty declares, "She does not feel she can leave her father. He would be alone in the house; that is to say, without family there. And she will not go off and leave him! I am sure that is it. Lord William would never ask her to stay. He would not want her to do that for his sake." Letty says emphatically, "She will not let anyone know the reason because it might get back to her father."

Hugh leans over to kiss her, and says, "You are the smartest woman I ever married!"

Letty responds, "I will be the *only* woman you ever marry." Addressing the others, Hugh asks, "So, what do we do?" With decisiveness, Letty states, "I have an idea. These two are made for each other. We cannot let this wonderful relationship just… dissolve. How many people in our society ever get the chance to marry for love? I shall make this my first priority." Then looking at Hugh's loving expression, she revises her statement, "Well, alright, my *second* priority!"

Robert leaves the home of his good friends, thankful for them. And, perhaps not quite as forlorn as when he arrived.

Several days later, Elizabeth and Letty have both received invitations to a ball being held, in two weeks, by their mutual friends, Viscount Wilcox and Lady Sarah. It is almost the end of the season, and Elizabeth should be completely recovered, by then. Letty will make sure that Robert attends, too. But he must take his own carriage. From Elizabeth, Letty has learned that her father has a standing appointment each week, with Doctor Brown. On one of these days, with his valet assisting him, Lord Addington comes out of the office, having finished his visit. Coincidently, he meets Letty, who just happens to be going inside. Since he has not seen Letty recently, they exchange greetings. Letty puts her hand on the Lordship's arm saying, "I was so surprised and saddened to hear that Elizabeth had refused Robert's proposal." She waits for his response and gets exactly what she was hoping for. Lord Addington is clearly just as upset. He states, "I truly felt that she had found someone she really loved, was happy to be with. And any numbskull could see he is a good man, who loves her, too. I am sure she is making a mistake and it breaks my heart to see it." He adds, "At my age, it will worry me now that she is not settled." Letty says she understands and looks sympathetic. He ends the conversation with, "Well, I must not keep you from your errands. It was good to see you. Tell Hugh I send regards."

Chapter 23

Letty has just confirmed it. The break was not His Lordship's idea; it was Elizabeth's. Her next step is to convince Elizabeth to accept Lady Sarah's invitation to the ball.

A week goes by, Elizabeth is in town, having just been meeting with the Community Harvest Committee. In a good mood, she decides to stop in at Doctor Brown's office. After asking about her father's general health, she questions where 'the other doctor' has been. Doctor Brown responds, "Oh, he left."

Elizabeth's face drops. The happiness is gone from her eyes. "Left for where?" she asks politely. "He left town; said he was doing research somewhere." The doctor answers. Looking at the door, he sees people come in. "Did he say when he will be back?" she continues. "No, he did not. My next patient is here; I will have to end this conversation. Thank you for stopping in and take care of yourself."

Feeling sadder than she could even admit, Elizabeth leaves and slowly, wearily, heads home. That night she has dinner in her room. *"What have I done?"* She asks herself.

A few days later, Lady Letitia and Lady Elizabeth are in town, shopping together. Letty has commissioned a seamstress to fashion a Christening outfit as a gift, for her new niece. The real reason she wanted to spend some time with Elizabeth happens when they have stopped for coffee. Letty orders tea, then says to Elizabeth, "Did I tell you I saw your father, a few days ago?" "No, you did not. You came to call?" Elizabeth asks. Letty answers, "Oh, I saw him in town. We were going right by each other, when I stopped to say 'hello.' I must say he looked a little dejected. I am sure he has not said anything to you, but I think he took your refusal of Robert quite hard." "Really, I do not understand." Elizabeth says, looking confused. Letty explains, "Well, you see, I think he felt contented to know that you were going to be settled with a good man like Robert. He would not have to worry about you. He likes Robert; he was happy that his daughter was going to marry someone she loves." Letty went on, "I will tell you; some fathers will marry a daughter off to anyone who has enough money. Luckily, our fathers are not like that because they love us. My father would have utterly despaired if Hugh had not come along." Trying to keep the topic on a light note, Letty continues as if she has just realized something, "Oh my goodness! Do you think that is why your father has been so downcast, lately? He is almost as dispirited as you are," she finishes dramatically, "That is it! He is worried about your future; that is what is making him almost ill!" Satisfied with her charade, Letty states, "Mmm, I am actually beginning to like tea more and more."

As the night of the ball approaches, Letty asks Elizabeth to attend the ball, as a favor, and Elizabeth agrees because Letty is truly her best friend. Once, again, Hugh and Letitia bring the carriage and give Elizabeth a ride. Once again, Elizabeth is quiet. When they arrive, Elizabeth notices there is an extra seat at their table. Not interested, she does not even question it.

On her way to get some punch a male guest asks her to dance. Remembering her manners, she says, politely, "Yes."

After the dance, while she is standing off to the side, she hears a voice close behind her say, "Elizabeth?" She straightens, recognizing it, even from a single spoken word. It is Robert. Fearing to move in case it was just her mind playing tricks, she stays still. He moves around slowly toward the front of her so that they are face to face. Looking into his eyes, tears well up to blur her vision. Quietly, he takes her arm, gently guiding her out onto the large patio for some air. He thinks she may faint. Worry shows on his face, "Are you alright?" he asks. She responds, "I am now," and gives him that beatific smile of hers.

Once again, he gives her his handkerchief. Not knowing what to say, both are quiet. But both of them know everything will be all right from now on. In a few moments, he asks her to dance. It is a new style of dance, called a slow waltz. It is perfect because they get to hold each other. "I am sorry I was a little late getting here." Robert states softly, "I shall never be late to dance with you, again."

Hugh and Letty are also on the dance floor. Letty's eyes say that she has noticed them dancing; she is smiling behind Hugh's shoulder.

When the evening is over, Robert drives Elizabeth home. He tells her he will be at her house, after breakfast tomorrow morning. This time they will get it right. Elizabeth's heart is so full she cannot speak; she just smiles.

After Robert makes the announcement to Lord Addington that 'Yes,' he and Elizabeth are engaged, His Lordship is thrilled and opens a bottle of his best champagne. The three of them toast. Elizabeth can see how happy this news has made her father. "*How could I have been so wrong?*" she thinks. "*Well, it is not the first time I have asked myself that question; and it probably will not be the last. Heavenly Father, please give Robert lots of patience. He is going to need it.*"

Chapter 24

The next morning, after breakfast, Elizabeth sends a letter to her brother, John, telling him about her engagement. She and Robert have agreed that the wedding will be at her home, with only close family and friends in attendance. They were thinking mid-November, so that they would be back from their honeymoon before Christmas. Elizabeth writes. "But, there is something important that I would speak to you about. Let me know when you can come to the country for a visit. Robert and I will broach the subject with just the three of us."

John is very happy to hear the news. Never quite sure what the problem was the day he saw her leave the room in hysterics, he had decided to withdraw from any contact with either of them. He figured the issue would sort itself out, or…it would not. Thankfully, it did.

It is the beginning of summer and even though the wedding will be a small one by all standards, there is still much to do. Tomorrow, she will go into London to see that nice young man at the print shop for invitations and print material for the Autumn Market Faire. *What was his name? Ben? That was it!*

The following day, Letty is going with Elizabeth to town to the dressmaker to have a wedding dress made. She will also get some new gowns, shoes, nightgowns and linens. Letty will need some new clothes, also. She ordered a very special gown to wear to the wedding and three everyday dresses from the dressmaker. Over coffee, Letty tells Elizabeth her happy news; she is with child. The doctor says she is due in January. Elizabeth is ecstatic for her and states, "Were there ever two happier women?"

"I have asked our local vicar to perform the ceremony; he was happy to do so. The ceremony and wedding reception will both take place at the manor. I explained to the vicar that Lord Addington is still recovering from being ill and the winter air would not be good for him. That is as far as I have gotten with the preparations until today. Oh, Letty, I cannot tell you how happy I am!" Elizabeth finishes.

Robert has been working on the final preparations for the conference entitled, 'Childbed Fever: The Disease and Its Considerations.' He has coordinated this along with three other doctors and, in spite of their qualms, asked several midwives to add their experiences, too. Almost all of the medical community in and around London has been invited. It is slated for the beginning of July, just before everyone leaves London for the summer. The day of the presentation comes. The main speaker is Dr. William Smellie, a physician and medical teacher who has kept detailed notes on hundreds of deliveries he has performed. Robert introduces Dr. Smellie saying, "After practicing in his hometown of Lanark, Scotland, he expanded his practice to London. Many inroads have been made in the delivery of infants.

Indeed, we have addressed several conditions which affect the health and safety of the mother and infant. There are still certain practices, such as the use of implements, cleanliness, and more important, information and record keeping about unsuccessful births." Robert asks the paramount question: "Why are cases of childbed fever, where the mother develops pain and fever one to two day after giving birth, then dies on the third day still occurring? Records are showing incidences of eighteen to twenty percent of women in the ward of the new lying-in hospital of London are still dying after giving birth. Clearly, nothing is being done to stop what the medical professionals are calling '*inflammation.*' Women, who come into the hospital healthy, before and during pregnancy, should not die after giving birth to a normal infant!" Robert adds, "I submit to you that if records were kept by midwives, they would show a lower mortality rate throughout their careers than what the hospital wards are showing now." Dr Smellie asserts, "Some possibilities could be, a midwife is only attending one woman at a time, unlike the hospital doctor who attends a pregnant woman after seeing a dozen other patients, bloodied and having different maladies. Also, midwives keep the mother and bedding, along with the midwife's hands very well cleansed. Medical science is learning a lot. There is still much to learn." He continued, "Perhaps the way we might learn, together, would be to keep details of our experiences and sharing them with the medical community? We would know where successful maternal care is happening and learn where it is not. Something we all need to think about! Thank you." Dr. Smellie concludes the presentation. Some questions and discussion follows. Finally, Robert brings the event to a close by saying, "The proof of the information and the ideas proffered today will be a rise in the number of successful births and healthy mothers."

Chapter 25

Later, that evening, Robert thinks to himself, "*Tomorrow, I will go into London and get fitted for several new suits.*"

Elizabeth tells John that all the invitations have gone out; she was happy to add the names of a few people that he wanted to have there. She also explains to John, in broad strokes, her idea of having both she and Robert continue to live and work at Addington Manor after they are married. She wants to keep an eye on their father for as long as she can, as long as is needed. She says this by way of asking John's permission; because he will be next in line as owner of the estate. She does not want to do anything that would ill-affect him. They will discuss this at his convenience.

John has written to Elizabeth, wishing her the best on her engagement. He is just finishing up a large and important case and will soon go before the Admiralty Court of the High Court. He continues, "It is a tribunal with jurisdiction over maritime law. That includes shipping, materials, and sea laws… things like that" He also writes, "A, Ronald Taylor, came to see me to explain a predicament and ask my advice about suing". John recounts, "It seems that together, he and a partner, own the shipping company called the Taylor Shipping Line. His father bought this trans-Atlantic route that goes from Georgia, in the colonies, to London, England. Their ships carry materials, tobacco, lumber, and sometimes a few passengers. The route proved so valuable to England, that King George the First entitled the father with a barony, if the shipping route stayed profitable and in the family's name. The father has passed on, but his two children now carry on the business. When one of their ship's contractors refused to pay them for the delivered goods, and it was a sizeable load, the two owners had to borrow money to cover costs and make sure the crew was paid upon landing. It seems the contractor likes to place wagers now and again; when he was drunk, he placed his manifest of goods as collateral for the bet. The owners of the shipping line have refused to allow the cargo to be off-loaded until it is paid in full." He indicates that, "One party has no money to pay for the goods; the other party will not pay because he says the goods now belong to him!"

John says in the letter, "I told the ship owners their best recourse was to petition the court to take ownership of the unpaid goods, in lieu of payment; then sell the goods to recoup their losses. The hearing is next week. I will meet both partners at court." He finishes, "After that, I would love to spend some time with you, Father, and your fiancé."

The posters, leaflets, and large banner have arrived from the print shop in London, for the Community Autumn Faire, scheduled for the last week in September. Posters will go up all over the area. The banner will be hung across the main street in town. The event is only five weeks away; the time will go fast. Elizabeth and the committee members are hard at work creating some decorations for inside the building. Villagers are starting to bring their handmade items to the community building, to be stored inside. Members are preparing food to be sold that day. Tables and chairs are being loaned from the church; a trio of musicians will play as people walk around. A special tribute, honoring the town's First Fire Company, will be presented to the men, and a plaque will be erected right outside the building.

A week before the case is to be presented at court John makes a visit to the office of Taylor Shipping Line, to go over last minute details. As he enters the office, a secretary is at a desk, covered with bills of lading, account information, and shipping schedules. She tells him to go on into the office, and she follows with a paper and pen, to take notes. Ronald Taylor introduces her as Katherine. John, smiles at her, bowing politely. When John is convinced that he has all pertinent information and necessary copies, he confirms the date and time that the partners should meet at the courthouse. Finished, he says goodbye and travels back to London. For reasons he cannot quite understand, he is 'smitten' with the appearance and efficiency with which the secretary handled the business! His personal belief is that women are capable of much more than society allows them. Lovely smile, too. Her approach to her work reminds him of his sister's, even the way she works, always wanting to understand things and do them correctly. *"Oh well, perhaps I have been working too hard. Still, she has a charming smile,"* he admits.

Chapter 26

In August most of the nobility have left for the comfort of their estates in the country, to get away from the smells of summer in London. Lord Bromley and Lady Letitia have invited many of their friends for a picnic on the grounds of their country estate. Windows and doors have been opened for extra air flow onto the patio. Food and drinks are set up inside. Tables and chairs are on the patio, lawn games, like bowling, are available and music fills the air. Comfortable chairs under canopies and trees create a relaxed atmosphere. Hugh keeps a diligent eye on Letitia since she is now about four months along. Elizabeth and Robert are never far from each other's side. Lady Sarah, with some instructions from her husband, Edmund, is trying her hand at archery. Within seconds, guests have vacated themselves from anywhere near the archery area of the garden. After lunch, when guests are reappearing in the garden, the bow and arrow are mysteriously missing.

The following Monday, John meets Ronald Taylor and Katherine in a small conference room, down the hallway from the courtroom. When John enters, he sees the two of them and asks Ronald, "Where is your business partner? It is important that he be here." Katherine responds, "I am the business partner. My brother and I own and run this business, together. I hope that is all right with you." Stammering, John says, "Yes, of course. It is just that it was not made clear when we were introduced and, well, I have nothing against women running businesses. My sister manages my father's estate, very well." It is only then that he begins to notice a smile breaking out from beneath her stern demeanor. He realizes she was playing with him. He smiles and thinks, "...*a sense of humor too!*"

After almost two hours of the case being heard, the verdict is declared. Since the passage for the goods was not paid for as contracted, the goods now belong to the Taylor Shipping Line. They are permitted to dispose of them as they wish. Award is to the plaintiff. Case closed. There is some court paperwork that needs to be signed. Then, Katherine hugs her brother. John says to Katherine, when they are outside, "I noticed your desk was quite full of work that needs to be done. If you ever have, even a short time, to engage in conversation, I should like to call on you, with your family's permission." Smiling broadly, she answers, "I would like to know more about you and get your measure. And that would be the best way to do it. I will be home Sunday afternoon." Responding, John says, "I will look forward to it." He thanks them both, shakes Ronald's hand and walks off smiling, waiting for Sunday.

John writes a brief note to Elizabeth stating that his court case is finished, and he will be at the manor Friday evening, after work.

Friday evening comes and Lord Addington, Elizabeth, Robert, and John have just enjoyed a wonderful meal and are sitting quietly, with an after-dinner drink. Since there is only one lady present and she would not leave the men just because they are having their brandy, the conversation continues. John has explained the case he finished, recently; but he does not mention Katherine to them, not yet. He is aware of the barn fire and asks for more details. Elizabeth tells him about the fire; and how well the new fire company responded. Intentionally, she leaves out the part about her going into the barn. Robert's eyes are fixed on her throughout the story. A smile lurks just below his countenance. To his credit, he remains silent on the matter of her saving the horse.

Perhaps because of the brandy, their father discloses an increasing concern of his. He tells them that he is forgetful at times. Yesterday, he forgot his valet's name which embarrassed him because it was evident to the valet. Last week, he was walking the grounds and for a little while, forgot where he was. The gardener happened to be passing by and pointed him toward the house. He divulged this honestly, yet sadly. John says, "We have an idea that we think would help everyone here. And I think you will like it. At least I hope you will! But, for now, it is late and we have all had a busy day. I, for one, would like to retire. Together, we shall go over the whole plan tomorrow, after breakfast. For tonight, sleep well, knowing that there is a plan." He asks his father, "If you are also going up, may I be of some assistance?" The three leave the room and head upstairs: William, John, and of course Leo, loping behind.

Chapter 27

Robert and Elizabeth are left alone in the dining room. Robert gestures to the brandy decanter, asking, ”Would you care for a little brandy? I noticed that you did not have any earlier.” She responds, “Yes, tonight, I think I will have one. Thank you.” Gazing at her with undisguised love and longing, he confesses, “I am looking forward to the time when we will be alone, together.” Elizabeth says smiling, “Well, we will hardly be alone in a place this size!” Robert stares at her intently. “You know what I mean.” Her face turns slightly red, telling him she feels the same. “I better go now or the staff will talk. But first, kiss me.” He walks over to where she is seated and puts his hand out to her. She stands up, so close their bodies are touching. When he kisses her, she cannot keep from wrapping her arms around him and leaning into him. Finally he says, “Yes, I better go now! I will see you tomorrow morning.”

When the four of them have finished their breakfast, the group gathers in the privacy of the library. John lays out the subject by way of a proposal to their father. Mindful of the respect that is owed and the condition of his father's health, John explains it as if they were clearly asking the Lord's permission. “Simply put,” John says, “Elizabeth and Robert, for about a year, would like to stay on and live at the estate.” Continuing in a softer, yet serious tone, “Elizabeth feels comfortable here and wants to continue to learn and keep her hand in the activities going on in the village. Robert certainly would not mind because the manor is closer to his work in London, where he would like to continue his medical research a little while longer also, Westerbrook Estate is having several of the rooms painted, redecorated, and new window hangings commissioned." John finishes by saying to his father, "But, this plan would only proceed if you would approve of having Elizabeth and Robert living here, for a while. So, we are asking for your thoughts on this. Of course, you need not decide right away. You can take as much time as you need or you can say 'no', right now, and we will not mention it again. Totally up to you. Did you want time to think it over?" John asked, carefully.

"Are you mad !" His Lordship exclaims, jolting everyone a bit. "I do not need time to think this over. I love the idea!" Lord William speaking with sparkling eyes says, "I would have the best of both worlds: I would get to see my daughter every day and I would be satisfied knowing that whatever happens, she is well settled to a good man. To tell you the truth, I thought something dreadful had happened, and I steadied myself to hear it. This is heartwarming news to hear, indeed!" In spite of the fact that it was, by most standards, a bit early in the day, they all had some champagne. Three of them thought they heard His Lordship whistling as he left the room. But each thought they must have been mistaken.

Later that day, Letitia and Elizabeth go into London to pick up their dresses from the dressmaker.

Robert goes to his estate and talks with his brother. John tries to keep his mind on his work, but can only think, *"Tomorrow is Sunday, and I will see Katherine."*

Finally, the day arrives that all the villagers and area townsfolk have been waiting for, the Autumn Faire. Yesterday, tents were set up. Early this morning, the cart brought over the tables and chairs from the church. Inside the community building, tables are wiped, decorative cloths are put on them, the committee places food items on the assigned tables and each person who signed up to bring handmade items is setting out their wares. Coffee and cider are set up, as well. Everyone knows that all of the extra proceeds will go toward fire company equipment. By mid-morning, the village is full. People are looking at homemade food, tools, clothing, shoes, quilts, garden plants, and more. In a far corner, pasture animals are for sale.

It is a beautiful day, so some are resting and eating at the tables outside. Some are happy to see friends and acquaintances and some make new friends, just by talking about what they made or are selling. Charles Young, a village woodworker, made a hand-cart that is especially useful on a farm and he is taking orders from farmers to make more.

Just before the lunch food comes out, everyone is asked to gather for an announcement. Elizabeth calls the names of the firemen and asks them to come forward. They are totally surprised when they are given awards for their bravery and selflessness. Also, Elizabeth has arranged for a money stipend to be given to each of these men, from an 'anonymous donor.' Robert had worked tirelessly all day and is now leaning against the wall with arms crossed, listening. He has been watching all this and is thinking," *This adorable woman is going to be my wife! What did I ever do to deserve that?"* He cannot keep from smiling!

The faire ends in early evening. Any leftover food is offered to workers to take home. Groups get busy to do the designated clean-up. Working together, it does not take long. In a little over an hour, the community building and the grounds are empty. Except for the banner still hanging across Main Street and the new plaque for firefighters hung on the wall, you would not think anything had happened here. But everyone will remember this day!

Chapter 28

The following week, Elizabeth receives an invitation to lunch with Lady Mary Wortley-Montagu at her London residence. Friends since they were first introduced, Elizabeth is excited and interested to speak with Lady Mary. On the day of the luncheon, Elizabeth realizes that she is the only guest. Delighted to see each other, the two women hug affably and quickly fall into a comfortable and affectionate demeanor. A table for two has been set for their lunch in the drawing room, where they can be undisturbed. Not one to stand on ceremony, Lady Mary pours wine for each of them from the sideboard table. Handing a glass to Lady Elizabeth, they move to sit in large, comfortable chairs that are perfect for conversing. Starting with a subject they are both familiar with, Lady Mary begins with a light, social topic of their experiences at court. Sometimes laughing, sometimes scowling, they regale each other with personal tales of being a member in the Court's Maids of Honor.

Lunch is served and the conversation is deferred. After a delicious lunch, the ladies move back to the chairs, where they are enjoying coffee. To Elizabeth's surprise, Lady Mary, once again, renews the subject of ladies at court; but, this time, with a more serious tone.

Mary tells Elizabeth, "I invited you here for a specific reason, not just to have lunch and chit-chat." Now, she has Elizabeth's full attention. Mary continues, "King George is not in the best of health and George the Second will follow, sooner rather than later, I suspect. You should know that when he and Princess Caroline become King and Queen, she will want you back at court."

Mary is careful to notice the look on Elizabeth's face at the mention of this. She elaborates, "She was fond of you as one of her attendees; I suspect she will 'invite' you back to court to resume your position. By then, you will probably have married; she will be the Queen. She gave you permission to leave court once; but, as Queen, she will not do it again. When she tells you to come to court, you will not have a choice." Mary sips her coffee giving Elizabeth a chance to process this information. "You know that being in the Queen's company is an all-consuming position. Your life will not be your own; Robert will have nothing to say about it. In addition, this position may last for many years. That may be exactly what some ladies want; but I do not see you as one of those. Nor do I see Robert, as a married man, without his wife by his side." Elizabeth slowly puts her coffee cup on the side table. Recognizing the look of enormous unease that has come over her friend, Mary moves to kneel in front of her; taking Elizabeth's hands in her own Mary says, "I think the world of you and Robert! I want nothing to happen that would interfere with your happiness. I tell you this because, as someone who knows a lot about court life, I can see what might be coming. I want you to be prepared. And…be able to consider possible options for your future, while you still have the time." Mary continues, "I considered not mentioning this to you, but as a friend, I felt I needed to tell you, so that you and Robert would be able to make your own decision. I hope I did the right thing!" Elizabeth and Mary both stand. Trying to keep her emotions in check, Elizabeth gives her friend a long, meaningful hug. Words are not needed. Each woman understands the importance of this conversation.

On the ride home, Elizabeth knows that she must share the news with Robert, as soon as possible.

That night after dinner, when they are alone in the dining room, Elizabeth re-tells the whole story of her conversation with Lady Mary Wortley-Montagu. Robert is not as surprised as Elizabeth was. She acknowledges, "I had some time to think, on the ride back home. The enormity of what you would have to give up, if you married me and this actually happened, would be more than I could bear. You would not think that was any kind of a life and neither would I. I had to tell you, as soon as I learned about this so you would have time to reconsider…maybe, change your mind…if you wanted." Elizabeth told him, looking down at her hands. Robert states, "You are right! This would be no kind of life for us." She looks up at him, waiting to hear his next words that would break her heart. Instead, he says, "So, we must look into the possibility of making new lives for ourselves, if this comes to fruition. The only thing I know for certain is that having you in my life and being able to practice medicine are things I will never give up." He comes to sit next to her. Taking her shoulders in his hands, looking at her intently, he says, " Elizabeth, consider this new information a good thing. Remember the saying, 'forewarned is forearmed.' And *always* remember, how much I love you." He kisses her, deeply, just to remind her.

When Robert leaves he makes a mental note to contact his lawyer and talk to his brother about this news. When he has an appointment with the lawyer, he will take Elizabeth with him.

Chapter 29

The next morning while having breakfast, Elizabeth receives a letter from John. She opens it and explains the gist of it, to her father. She tells him, "He writes about someone special that he has met. He recounts the story of the court case he had recently, involving two owners of the trade ship who were not paid for their cargo. He says that one of the owners was a woman named, Katherine Taylor. She and her brother own the shipping line." Elizabeth says, "Imagine that!" She continues, "John has called on her; they have gone out walking; had a few meals, together, with her brother. He states he finds her 'intelligent, business minded, humorous, and, perhaps, a little interested in him, too.'" Elizabeth stops to give her father a surprised glance. Continuing, she relates, "He writes to know… "if Robert and I would be able to meet them in London, for dinner soon?" Elizabeth tells her father that she is happy for him and curious about someone who could finally get John away from his law books to enjoy life a little more. She declares to her father, "If John likes Katherine, I will, too!"

Elizabeth writes back that they can meet in one week. John will make reservations for them at the best restaurant in London.

Elizabeth writes to Lady Mary W.M. thanking her for the lovely lunch and telling her that she has spoken to Robert, regarding their conversation. They are both extremely grateful for her insight and 'advice.' They will also be looking into options that might be available to them. And, to please, let them know about anything else she might hear that would be helpful.

Robert has made plans to go to his estate and spend a couple of days with his brother.

He has also received confirmation about the plans he made for the honeymoon. Since they will only be gone for three weeks, they decided to spend the time in the south of France, on the coast, visiting small towns in the surrounding area. The decision not to do a long honeymoon was something they had both agreed upon, in light of her father's health.

Elizabeth and Letty are in the drawing room, going over the wedding R.S.V.P.s and seating arrangements. The wedding is now just three weeks away; the days are getting busier for the entire household.

After a few days, Robert has returned from visiting his estate. He has made special legal and financial arrangements adding his brother, Stephen, as co-owner to an account owned by Robert. He informed Stephen, that should he and Elizabeth ever move out of England, the solicitor has been instructed to execute a document, passing the title of Earl, the estate, along with all his earthly goods in England to Stephen.

Robert has withdrawn a very sizeable amount of cash that will be kept handy, in case of emergency. Robert has asked Stephen for strict secrecy on this subject.

Robert will see his brother and sister-in-law, Amelia, at the wedding.

Tonight, they are having dinner with her brother, John, and Katherine Taylor. They will also have to let John know of their 'optional' plans, but not tonight. Tonight is for socializing! John has taken his carriage to the Taylor's home to pick up Katherine. He has seen her on a number of occasions, but he is not prepared for the striking beauty who sweeps slowly down the stairs, her eyes fixed on him. Hair swept up, dressed in a rose-colored silk gown, with pearls around her neck, she is a vision. Seeing the reaction she was hoping for, Katherine begins a slow, broadening smile.

To anyone watching, these are two love birds, staring and smiling at each other. "Good evening, John," she says, using his familiar name. He cannot say anything; he is too busy smiling. Seeing no maid servant around, he steps in to help her with her hooded cloak.

The carriage takes Robert and Elizabeth to London, where they meet John and Katherine, at the restaurant. They are already seated when John and Katherine arrive. Robert immediately stands, bows slightly during the introduction. Then, John introduces the women, "Lady Katherine, may I introduce my sister, Lady Elizabeth Spencer, of Addington Manor." Elizabeth says, "How do you do? Please, call me Elizabeth or Beth." Then he introduces Robert, who says, "How do you do." And politely bows. Looking at John's face, Robert thinks to himself, *"I know that look well."* After ordering drinks, Elizabeth says to Katherine, "John tells me you and your brother are owners of a shipping trade route. That sounds very exciting!" Katherine responds, "Well, 'exciting' may not be the best word, but it has its moments. You just never know what is going to happen. Last year, we had a ship that was sighted by pirates, off the coast of Georgia, in the colonies. It was only able to escape because a brief gale wind blew the other ship off course. And, of course, John probably told you about the case we brought to him, when we needed to recoup payment for a cargo we delivered. He was referred to us because he knew contract law. You should have seen him in court!" For a moment, John thought to himself, *"Robert and I need not have come this evening. The ladies have carried almost the entire conversation between themselves* "Then he realizes, *"I would not have wanted to miss this for the world. Just met, and they seem like longtime friends."* Katherine states, "I understand that you two are to wed, soon. How did you meet?" Robert and Elizabeth exchange looks. He says, "Would you like to tell her, or should I?" raising his brow, slightly. Elizabeth, realizing the story would be better coming from her, tells him, "I will explain; you do not do it properly." And, she proceeds to improvise the carriage accident… a bit. Concluding, she says, "By the end of the dinner party, he had redeemed himself enough, with his dancing and politeness. I decided I should give him another chance and I agreed to see him, again. So, here we are!" Robert's expression shows one of humor and enough strength of character to remain silent. After a few minutes of perusing the menu, the group orders dinner. Later, after enjoying a wonderful meal, the women learn a few other things that show they have much in common: neither can sew, play an instrument or sing. Elizabeth says she can find the kitchen, with help. Katherine says she can easily find her kitchen, but when she gets there, she pretends she cannot cook." She elaborates, "My brother is actually a very good cook, and he likes to do it. So, I say, why should I deprive him of that? However, when we have guests over, we both say that I cooked the meal. It saves a lot of silly questions."

Ending the meal with coffee, and brandy for the gentlemen, they eventually part company. All four of them smiling, having had such a delightful evening.

Chapter 30

In the carriage, Elizabeth says to Robert, "I know we have only just met her and the invitations have already gone out, but we simply must get John to invite her to the wedding. I hope you agree!" Robert replies, "Yes, I actually do." She snuggles closer to him. When Robert gets back to his flat in London, there is a letter for him. It is from his brother, Stephen. He writes that, "… Amelia has delivered a baby girl! The delivery was about three weeks earlier than expected; both are doing well." Stephen is sorry to say that they may have to miss his wedding because Amelia and the baby will not be fit to travel in the cold weather. If they continue to do well, he may venture to come by himself and just stay overnight. He regrets the imposition but is sure Robert will understand. *"Of course, I understand!"* Robert thinks to himself and proceeds to his desk to write a note of congratulations.

It is the day before the wedding. The guest count numbers forty-two. The manor is strewn with white flowers and greenery, furniture has been moved to accommodate the entire group standing during the ceremony, in the living room. The dining room is festooned with lush garlands and white candles. The dining table is exquisitely set for forty-four wedding guests plus the bride and groom. The fine china and tableware are being used. A small bar area is set up in the foyer, which will be initiated after the service is completed. Footmen are active outside as the carriages arrive. Lord William is being helped by his valet. Fiona is assisting Elizabeth while Letitia is relaxing in the room; she feels a bit oversized from the pregnancy. The vicar, Richard Agar, has arrived and is in the library, putting on his official cassock and collar. The musicians are playing softly. Robert is changing in the men's quarters. Hoping that his brother will be able to attend, he has asked if John would be good enough to be his best man, if needed. John has picked up Baron Taylor and Lady Katherine, who are also attending. Last minute items are being brought into the dining room, while everyone gathers in the large living room.

The head housekeeper is told that the bride is ready; she sends word to the groom and best man to take their places. The music stops as a signal that the wedding music will begin. The vicar moves into position. The head housekeeper returns to Elizabeth, telling her that everyone is in place. A knock on the front door shows that Stephen has arrived, just in time to take his place at his brother's wedding. They smile at each other. The pianist begins to play Bach's *Prelude in C Major*. All eyes turn toward the staircase. Elizabeth, looking radiant, descends slowly, confidently, toward her father, who is waiting at the bottom of the stairs to take her hand. The hush of the guests is marked only by their intake of breath at seeing how beautiful she looks. As they reach the doorway to the living room, they stop, momentarily. Letty is behind them, ready. Walking slowly toward the vicar, and her new life, Elizabeth will remember her eyes on Robert and his never leaving hers. With their family and closest friends around them, Robert and Elizabeth pledge their hearts and bodies to each other so that their joy may be doubled and their sorrow halved. Each of them pledges to the other their support and loyalty. Even if one does not always understand, they will always trust. Using the library as the vestry, the vicar and couple leave for a moment, and go into the library to sign the official register. While they are gone, the musicians play, *Trumpet Tune*, by Clarke. Upon returning, the vicar offers a prayer for the couple and asks friends and loved ones to support and help guide Elizabeth and Robert as they start their lives, together. The final pronouncement is made and the ceremony concludes. Elizabeth and Robert turn, in unison, to face their supportive and loving congregation.

The musicians start the celebration playing Vivaldi's *Spring*, as the couple walk together toward the doorway, where they form a receiving line to greet all their guests, who shower them with admiration and accolades. All are socializing and enjoying punch, brandy, and the music. As Elizabeth becomes engulfed in a crowd of ladies, Robert takes the time to introduce Lord William and John to his brother, Stephen. John introduces Ronald and Katherine to family. Elizabeth sees John and quickly goes to greet Katherine and to meet her brother. Robert has just enough time to get two cups of punch before Lewis goes to Elizabeth to announce that the wedding breakfast is about to be served. She announces, "There are no place cards, so please sit wherever you like." Giving the punch cups to a waiter, Robert goes to Elizabeth and escorts her into the dining room.

Any extra wedding cake and appetizers will be sent downstairs, for the staff to enjoy.

Later, as the wedding reception comes to an end, Robert, Elizabeth, John, Katherine, and Ronald spend a little time together, in the library. Hugh and Letty, after making their excuses, left earlier as she was feeling tired. Lord William has gone to bed, feeling better than he has in a long time. Robert calls for the carriage and their cases are brought down to be loaded.

It is early evening, and John gets ready to leave with Katherine and Ronald.

Elizabeth goes upstairs to change for the trip. Fiona, who is a little melancholy, becomes teary-eyed as she says "goodbye" to her mistress. The driver and coach are ready to take them to the best hotel in London. Lewis and the head housekeeper are downstairs, by the front door, waiting to wish Elizabeth and Robert a Bon Voyage. Eventually, they board the coach. As it pulls away, Robert gives Elizabeth a look that is filled with yearning. She leans into him, giving him a kiss that holds a promise of things to come. He is content for now. So begins their lives together.

In the morning they will board a ship, cross the channel, and head toward the south of France.

Chapter 31

Before His Lordship comes down for breakfast, the decorations have already been removed, furniture restored to original places, and the flowers sent to the local hospital.

Lord William feels colder, already. He thinks, *It is going to be a long three weeks.*

John is hard at work, in London and spends Sundays with his father. Still, he is conscientious about staying in touch with Katherine. She and her brother have turned down several contracts for their ships to carry human cargo. They are adamant that their ships do not traffic in the slave market, no matter what happens. They plan well and carry enough merchandise to make a good profit. The number of passengers who are going to the colonies has increased. Some return to England, most do not.

It is the latter half of November, and the weather is getting colder. Before she left, Elizabeth made sure that Rose Burn and her family will always have wood piled in their yard for the winter.

King George the First is having a winter party at the palace, in London. Invitations have gone out to many of the nobility, including the Earl of Addington and his son Viscount John Spencer of Shelbourne. The King is not always in England; he does not usually attend cabinet meetings. So, many who wish to be noticed will be in attendance. John and Lord William have discussed this. Lord William's health precludes him from attending, but he feels that John should certainly make an appearance. Reluctantly, he agrees. His law firm has also encouraged him to make his presence known. He has asked Katherine to accompany him. She feels honored and is interested in going. Not one to spend her money on things she will only use sporadically, she nevertheless, has a new dress commissioned. Also expecting to attend, will be Lord and Lady Berwick, along with their daughters, Lady Pricilla and Lady Margery.

The night of the party arrives. John has picked up Katherine, and they head toward St. James Palace, the King's residential house, which is not far away. After a long reception line, in which John introduces Lady Katherine to the King, they move into the ballroom. As they move around the room, John sees neighbors and club members that he has not seen in many months. Always introducing Katherine, they have brief conversations and then move on. John offers to get some punch and asks Katherine to wait nearby until he returns. When John leaves, Lady Pricilla moves over to talk to Katherine before she has a chance to sit down. "You look familiar; but I cannot place the name," Pricilla says to Katherine. Katherine responds, "I am afraid you have me at a disadvantage. Have we met?" "It is hard to hear with all these people. Let us just step over here, for a minute," Pricilla says. Taking Katherine's arm somewhat firmly, she guides her to a small out of the way alcove saying, "To answer your question, 'No', we have not exactly met; we do know someone in common." Katherine looks concerned and her eyes begin to look around for John. She realizes that he will not be able to see her, in this small alcove area. Noticing that Katherine has become distracted looking for John, Pricilla's countenance becomes decidedly unfriendly. When Katherine looks back at Pricilla, she is immediately on guard. Pricilla, still holding her arm, says, "We both know John Spencer, Viscount of Shelbourne. In fact, John and I are engaged. We have been seeing each other for well over a year, now. I was supposed to meet him here; so, I am wondering why you are here, walking around with him." Moving menacingly closer to Katherine's face, she continues, "I suggest you leave this place…quickly."

"And I suggest you take your hand off my arm," Katherine says in a steady, hard voice. John is standing by the seating area, holding two cups of punch, looking for Katherine. She walks away from Pricilla, toward John, who brightens when he sees her. Katherine tries to act as if nothing has happened; but the light-heartedness of the evening is gone. After two more dances, she asks John, "I am so sorry. I hope you will not mind too much if we leave early." John, wondering if she is unwell says, "Of course, I will have our coach brought around."

Signaling a footman, he tells him to get their coach. With an arm around her shoulder, John walks with her to the front foyer to retrieve their cloaks. She is quiet on the ride home. Upon arriving, he sees her to the door and she asks him to come inside for a few minutes. When they are in the drawing room, John surmises that something is amiss. He pours two glasses of brandy, handing one to Katherine. After a few minutes of silence pass, Katherine says, "I met your fiancée, tonight." John's brandy spurts out and he coughs. Katherine continues, "Do you know a Lady Pricilla Berwick?" From the look on his face she says, "Well, it appears that you do. She told me she was supposed to meet you there, tonight. Would you like to tell me about your relationship?" Feeling innocent of any forthcoming charges, John states emphatically, "First of all, there is no relationship! I met her through people at court. We spent a short time together. There was never any intention of a commitment because I realized we had nothing in common. I stopped calling on her." He continues, "That was months before I ever met you and agreed to take your case to court." Softly, he says. "Then I met you, and as far as I am concerned, there is no one else." Katherine relates, "John, all I wanted to do was slap her…but I knew that it was neither the time nor the place. I will tell you something, that Pricilla has quite a grip, for a Lady. I felt it when I moved to leave. I do not know what came over me!" John thinks he knows, but remains quiet. "Of course, I had the advantage. I am a businesswoman, used to dealing with all types." More softly she says, "I think I know you well enough. And I find you to be an honorable man. I did not believe her; but I was a bit frightened by what I wanted to do!" Finishing, she says, "So, there you are. That is the kind of person you are dealing with. I will understand if you do not want to continue seeing such a person." As she is looking over the rim of her glass, John can see that her eyes are smiling.

Chapter 32

Catastrophe avoided, John walks over to her, takes the glass from her and places it on the table. Putting his arms around her, he gently lifts her face up, and they kiss. It is as natural as it is shared in passion and longing. "I will never let anyone hurt you again," he hears himself say. "You had better not; I will take one of my brother's frying pans to you!" she states. John flirtatiously smiles and says, "Your brother will not always be around us." "Well, I shall have to think on that," she responds, with furrowed brow. Smiling, she kisses him, teasingly, but before she can release herself, he pulls her back and kisses her like she has never been kissed before.

"I would like to call on you, tomorrow morning, about ten o'clock, if you are available," John asks.

Katherine has a good idea of what this means and she responds playfully, "I think I could be at home, then." "Make sure you are!" John says in a mockingly stern voice. They both laugh. Neither will get much sleep, tonight.

Robert and Elizabeth will be home in three days; all of them will have much to talk about.

The day has arrived and Elizabeth and Robert are due home within the hour. A luncheon has been arranged for them with Lord William, John, and Katherine there, too. After hearing all about the newlyweds' trip, John will make his announcement that he and Katherine are engaged. He has brought a bottle of champagne to share. Then, he and Katherine will ride back to London. He has work to do and Katherine has plans to make. Besides, the arriving couple must surely be tired from their traveling and eager to settle in at home.

Elizabeth has sent a note to Letty's residence asking how she is and hoping she would not mind a visit in a couple of days.

When Elizabeth does visit Letty, she is a little taken back by her friend's obvious physical discomfort. Letty confesses to Elizabeth that she feels as big as a house and is having trouble getting up, sitting, and even sleeping. Elizabeth notices her drawn complexion and dark rimmed eyes, from lack of a good night's sleep. Elizabeth asks, "What does your doctor have to say?"

Letty responds, "He thinks I am making too much of it. He says he sees this happen a lot, with first time mothers. And speaking without any real concern, the doctor tells me, "The baby might be 'a little oversized'! So, even if this weather were not cold and damp, I would not be going anywhere." Conspiratorially, she says, "None of this to Hugh, though. He would only want to sit in the room with me and watch my every move." Not wanting to fatigue her friend any longer, Elizabeth leaves a gift that she has brought from France and goes home, slightly worried.

It is ten days before Christmas. Elizabeth has seen to it that a large tree has been brought in and set up in the foyer. While away, she read about different Christmas traditions in other cultures and is going to try some of them this year. Evergreens are brought in, and doorways and handrails are decorated. Decorations are given to the servants, for their own use, downstairs.

Tonight, she will tell Robert about the trouble Letty is having with the pregnancy; she does not look very well. Although he is not her doctor, he may have some advice to offer.

Elizabeth is also planning a party at the house, after Christmas, for the official announcement of John and Katherine's engagement. A happy celebration and an announcement! She should develop an invitation list and get that out tomorrow; then, she will begin wrapping gifts for the many estate workers.

Lord William asks Elizabeth to have Wrede, their agent, come and see him, in the library, after lunch. He explains to Elizabeth, "I was not able to get downstairs for the retirement party that the staff had for him; I want us to spend some time with him. And, I have a retirement 'gift' for him." "Certainly", she replies, "I will see that he is here at… shall we say, 3PM?"

At 3pm, Elizabeth meets Wrede as he is coming into the foyer. They walk to the library and find His Lordship seated comfortably, with a blanket on his lap and the fireplace going. William says brightly, "Wrede, my good man, come in! Come sit over here, where it is warm." Wrede sits in one of the wing-back chairs opposite William. A knock on the door and Lewis enters with a tray of liquors and glasses. He sets it down and leaves. Elizabeth says, "We have brandy, whiskey, and scotch. Which would you prefer?" Elizabeth continues, "I know that champagne is usually the drink of the moment; I also know you two, and I thought any of these drinks would be preferable."

Wrede says, "Once, again, your daughter is a quick learner." Pouring out drinks for each of them, she turns to her father. He lifts his glass in a salute to his friend and says, "To one of my most cherished colleagues, may your joys be many and your worries few. Cheers!" They talk for a few minutes about the present condition of the estate, the thoughtful changes Elizabeth has made, and the growing families of his sons. After a while, Lord William, pulls out an envelope and gives it to Wrede. With his eyes slightly glassy, he says, "Please accept this as a small token of my appreciation for the work of a most trustworthy and valued fellow worker."

Elizabeth has never seen Wrede at a loss for words. Fearing he may become emotional, Wrede only manages to say softly, "Thank you, sir. It has been my honor." They finish their drinks.

Chapter 33

Two days before Christmas and the snow starts falling. Elizabeth is enjoying a nice breakfast with her husband and father. Only two more items on her list need doing; she will finish them this morning. Their gardener has sent word, through the household, that he suspects the snow will keep falling through nightfall. Extra food is stocked inside and hay is available in the barn. The coach is always ready, since Robert never knows when a doctor might be needed.

The snow falls, all through the day, and into early evening. All chimneys are operating. His Lordship is huddled in a warm blanket, near his fireplace, with his dog. Elizabeth is rechecking the party planning list, and Robert is reading the most recent manual on midwifery procedures.

Just before dinner, there is an urgent banging on the front door. A young man, soaked from the heavy snowfall and panicked, asks to speak with 'the doctor'. Elizabeth and Robert come into the foyer to see what the commotion is all about. The boy blurts out, "Sir, I was told to come get you as quickly as possible. My mistress's time has come and she is in a bad way. Her own doctor's carriage got a broken wheel in the snow, and there's nobody to help her!" Robert tells, Lewis, "This boy is too wet to ride out. I am going to write an address down. Get a stable hand to go to this place and ask the midwife if she would come and help Doctor Barnett at Lord Bromley's estate, on Newcastle Road. Ask them to come as fast, and as safely as they can. And, have the coach brought around." He yells over his shoulder. Elizabeth takes a blanket from the drawing room and puts it over the boy's shoulders. Robert runs up the stairs to change his outfit, grab boots, and his black case. He is pulling on his winter cloak when the coach arrives out front. Elizabeth says to the boy, "You can go downstairs and have some hot soup." The boy, his fear evident, responds, "No, Miss, I have to go home to see about my mistress. She may need me, again!" Understanding, Elizabeth says, "All right then, you ride in the coach with the doctor. "Let us go!" Robert says, half running out the door.

Using the 2-horse coach for more stability, they move along steadily, if not quickly, through the snow.

It is already dark when they pull up to the front of the manor. Hugh is out in front, with a lantern as soon as he sees the coach enter the property. Footmen have placed additional lanterns on the roadway approaching the house. Robert jumps out, meeting Hugh on the stairs. The look of distress is clear on Hugh's face. *Something must be very wrong.* Robert thinks, to himself. Stripping off his cloak and hat, he follows Hugh to the bedroom. Letty looks pale and exhausted, but she smiles weakly, when she sees Robert. He tells her, "I am going to help out until your own doctor gets here. Is that alright?" she nods, lightly.

He tells the lady's maid, "I will need soap, a large pan of hot water, and clean linens, that can be torn up, if necessary." Taking off his jacket and rolling up his shirt sleeves, he washes his hands and arms thoroughly and dries them on the clean linen. It is about that time they hear banging on the front door. Hugh, thinking that it is the other doctor, goes downstairs. He opens the door to find an older woman, who is asking where the mother is. Robert is on the balcony and, not standing on ceremony, tells her to come up. Robert tells the maid to keep making hot water; they will need it all the time. Letty lets out a small cry of pain and distress. He tells Hugh to stay by his wife's head and talk encouragingly to her. The midwife is washing her hands, just as Robert begins to gently palpate Letty's stomach, to get an idea of the baby's position. He asks the midwife to do the same careful exam. They look at each other, both knowing that this is not a single birth; it is likely twins. Speaking to Hugh and Letty, Robert says, "It is very possible that you are having twins. Mrs. Beals and I are going to help deliver them. Do you understand?" Robert tells her, "The problem is that they are blocking each other from descending into the birth canal," Robert briefly explains to Letty and Hugh, "We have to move one of the babies into a delivery position; this may feel uncomfortable. Hugh, you will hold Letty's hand, while Mrs. Alice Beals helps me."

Robert has a difficult time deciphering the babies' positions for a moment, until he feels the back of one baby; then recognizes the head of the other twin, in a downward position. Slowly, after turning the body, so it faces downward, the mother's body takes over with labor contractions. After a while, the head crowns, but the baby does not move. Suspecting that the umbilical cord may be caught, he slowly turns the baby's head and, seeing the cord, manually pulls the cord to the other side of the baby's head, allowing the body to descend, unimpeded. Mrs. Beals takes the baby, after delivery, clears the mouth and throat. She wipes and cleans the newborn; presenting the baby to the parents, and announces, "You have a boy!" Robert tells them, "We are not done, yet." After palpating again, he realizes, this baby is in breach position. He tells Letty, "Other contractions are coming; try to hold off, if possible, until I can move the infant into head first position." With slightly more room, now, he can turn the infant properly. In a short time, a baby girl is delivered! Again, Mrs. Beals takes over care of the newborn from Robert, and hands the baby to the proud parents. Robert makes sure that everything else is taken care of. Switching places, Mrs. Beals tells everyone to leave the room for a moment, while she takes care of the mother. Letty is washed and helped into a clean night gown. The bed linens are stripped while she sits near the warm fireplace, holding her daughter. Hugh sits in another chair, staring and smiling at his son.

Relieved and glad the deliveries were successful and Letty is healthy, Hugh is feeling splendid, beyond words! He cannot possibly thank Robert and Mrs. Beals for what they have done. Hugh is well aware that if they had not come, Letty and the babies could have died.

Quietly, Hugh gives Mrs. Beals a very generous payment and his heartfelt thanks for her help, and wishes her and her family a Merry Christmas.

By the time Robert takes Mrs. Beals home and then arrives back at the manor, it is almost dawn. Tomorrow is Christmas!

Chapter 34

Elizabeth has waited all night in the overstuffed chair for Robert to come home.

When he walks in the front door, he gives her the wonderful news in two short sentences. They both go upstairs; feeling incredibly thankful, they fall into bed, exhausted.

The next day, two messenger carriers pass each other on the road. One is going to the Bromley estate. It is a note from Elizabeth, sending the happy couple love and best wishes on the birth of their twins. She hopes to see them soon, but will give the new mother a chance to rest, first.

The other rider is delivering a note to Addington Manor from Lord and Lady Bromley. It is addressed to Robert, Earl of Westerbrook. Words fail them! But, please, know that their hearts are full of love for their babies, because of him. And, they hope he will consent to be a godparent for the twins.

Three days after Christmas, the roads are clear and Robert and Elizabeth have a coachman take them to Westerbrook, Robert's estate in Sussex, to visit his family. Lord and Lady Barnett are thrilled to see them. After the luncheon, Elizabeth cannot wait to meet her little niece, Christine, named after Amelia's mother. She is almost sitting up, now, and has light brown hair and blue eyes, just like her father.

Stephen tells them he is positive she has her mother's voice, especially when she wants something. Husband and wife exchange smiles.

Elizabeth and Robert have brought the little one some outfits from France, which it seems, she will be wearing quite soon. Robert and Stephen take a short walk about the grounds of the estate, with Robert pointing out places where refurbishing and decorating will begin. Elizabeth has time to ask Amelia questions, which she would not do, when the men were present. When they return, Stephen and Amelia ask Elizabeth if she would consent to be the godmother for Christine. Elizabeth is honored to be asked. The Christening will be in the spring.

All four are aware of what might happen when George the First dies; but it is not spoken of, now.

Robert and Elizabeth arrive home only slightly late for afternoon tea.

Next week, the Holiday Engagement Party will take place. Elizabeth has met with Katherine and filled her in on who was invited, the menu, and general arrangements.

Elizabeth makes a short visit to see Letty and the twins. Letty is in the library when Elizabeth arrives, because it is warmer there. She has a lap robe on, and each of the twins is in a basket, on either side of her. A fire makes the room comfortable. Elizabeth is enchanted by the two newborns. As the conversation moves on, Elizabeth tells her about

Katherine and how John is more excited than she has ever seen him.

Letty says, "My only disappointment is that since the babies arrived earlier than expected, I will not be able to attend John's engagement party. "Elizabeth says, "We will have a small dinner party, in the spring, when the weather is nicer." Letty also confides, "I have a wet nurse. I wanted to nurse one of the babies, myself. I know women in our station do not do this. Hugh thought it was too much for me, but I was insistent. So, we switch the babies back and forth. I cannot explain the feeling of love and amazement that comes from nursing; but you will know it, when you have your own." Elizabeth is so happy for her friend.

On the night of the engagement party, the manor looks like a shining light in the dark night. Candles are lit everywhere, and piano music can be heard coming from the salon area.

Carriages are pulling up to the front and a light snow is falling. It is not going to last, because Elizabeth's gardener told her so. The receiving line contains Lord William, Elizabeth, Robert, John, and Katherine. Later, guests move about, congratulating Robert and asking them both about their recent travels. People share Christmas and family stories. John, too, is walking around with Katherine on his arm, introducing her to everyone. Lord William escorts Ronald, making introductions. Some guests have already met John's girlfriend at Elizabeth's wedding; most did not, because it was a small ceremony. Then, Lord William taps his glass to get everyone's attention. He encourages everyone to take a glass of champagne from the wait staff walking around. A toast is about to be made. John and Katherine have slowly moved toward William, so that they are standing next to him. He calls Ronald up who makes the announcement about his sister. Everyone smiles, raises a toast, and sips champagne. Clapping and congratulating John; they also give best wishes to Katherine, who looks especially lovely. Soon, dinner is announced. John and Katherine sit on either side of Lord William. Ronald is next to his sister; Elizabeth and Robert are seated at the other end of the table. Guests seem to be either surprised, impressed, or shocked when they learn that Katherine helps her brother run a shipping company. Katherine is aware of people's reactions, but thinks to herself," *John is both proud and in love with me; nothing else matters.* "And, this thought makes her smile broadly.

After dinner, the gentlemen stay in the dining room, smoking and talking. The ladies retire to the drawing room where coffee, tea, and small desserts are setup. There is much talk about these ladies' own weddings and plenty of advice for the fiancée. Lady Katherine gives the impression that she is interested in all of their opinions. Elizabeth knows Katherine is a Lady who will make her own choices. Lord William leaves the party, quietly slipping off to his room, too tired to stay.

At last, the party ends. John's coach has been brought around to the front. They thank Elizabeth and Robert for their hard work. Katherine and Elizabeth walk arm in arm to the door like lifelong friends, laughing at some of the comments made that evening.

And, just as the gardener predicted, the snow is barely visible.

Chapter 35

As January sets in, the days are cold and the sky is gray. If there is no reason to go outside, everyone is quite content to stay indoors. There is one trip that Elizabeth has on her schedule.

It has been weeks since she has visited the community building; and she is anxious to be brought up to date on events. Before going, she will go through their closets and see if there are extra blankets, bedding, coats, boots, and any other items that can be added to the exchange table. Those who have nothing to offer, may take what they need and bring items they can exchange in the springtime. Curiously, Elizabeth has come across a number of 'new' blankets and dozens of candles that she needs to get rid of; so she brings them to the community room for those in need. In a few months, she will introduce Katherine to these wonderful people. She will have to take her place as community board member, after the wedding.

During the second week in January, Lord William comes down with a cold and is required to stay in bed. His doctor has just visited again, and is concerned that his condition might be weakening him. Elizabeth has been attending to him. Lord William, on his good days, speaks almost in a whisper to Elizabeth, telling her how thankful he was to have two of the best children that any parent could want. He has had a full, productive life and is at peace with whatever will happen. Elizabeth is not ready to hear any of this. Robert, having witnessed this type of thing before, knows that William is preparing to say goodbye. He will send out a rider with a note to John today, telling him to be prepared and to come soon. Elizabeth stays in the room with her father all the time, now. Small meals are brought, for her, but she is rarely hungry. John arrives later that same day. The household has become very quiet. Elizabeth has pulled up a chair, next to her father. She is holding his hand; when, exhausted, she falls asleep. She is awakened by the dog, crying at her feet. Still holding his hand, she notices there is no need to worry anymore. Softly, she begins to weep; then sob, uncontrollably. John and Robert have been in chairs across the room and hear her. They allow Elizabeth a moment alone, to mourn near her father. Sorrowfully, John goes to tell Lewis to make the announcement to the staff, send word to the doctor, and notify Harrow's Funeral Home. Robert carefully goes to Elizabeth. Standing on feeble legs, she turns to him. He enfolds her in his arms; and in her grief and exhaustion, she leans against him, knowing instinctively she can rely on his support. He guides her out of the room, closing the door behind them. Elizabeth goes to her room and lies on her bed. Fiona enters to cover her with a blanket and stay in a chair nearby. Leo, coming from his master's room, pushing the door open with his nose, enters Elizabeth's room and lies down near her.

John goes to his own room to be alone, and quietly weep for his own loss.

Doctor Brown arrives. Robert meets him in the foyer. He will see Lord William first, for the official record. Then, he will see Elizabeth. John comes down the stairs slowly and greets the doctor. The doctor for the first time, refers to John as 'Your Lordship', since he has just become the Earl of Addington Manor.

A notice is written for the local paper, stating details of the service and that the wake will be at Addington Manor. John notifies Katherine and family members. Robert lets his brother know, and a notice is sent to the Township Committee, to let the villagers know. When the vicar hears of it, he tolls the church bell, slowly.

Robert goes into the bedroom to be with Elizabeth when Harrow's people arrive.

Harrow sets up the drawing room for the viewing, which will be held tomorrow. The doors are kept closed until then. Villagers, friends, staff, and coworkers will come to pay their respects. Families, including Katherine, Ronald and Robert's family will arrive beforehand. John has asked Elizabeth if she would mind, very much, if Katherine was included in the receiving line.

He tells her, "I know she is not family, yet. We are not married. But I would like to have her there with me; the villagers will get a chance to meet her, if that is alright with you. What do you say?" John sits down, elbows on his knees, head in his hands. Elizabeth says, "Of course, it is alright with me. You will be married in a few months; and I already think of her as a sister. I am sure she will be a big help." Seeing that John is taking this harder than she would have expected, Elizabeth goes over to him, and kneeling in front of him says,"I am so sorry, John. Your life has changed now, in immeasurable ways. I know you and Katherine will do an excellent job running the estate; Father will be proud of you, just as always." She gives him a big hug. Somehow, comforting someone else has helped Elizabeth to put her own sorrow aside, for the moment. She has responsibilities that must be taken care of and, she is ready. Elizabeth goes downstairs to the kitchen area, looking for the housekeeper and cook. Meeting with them she explains the plan, "Anyone of the staff wishing to pay respects can do so tonight, after their dinner. A few close family members will arrive after breakfast, tomorrow morning. Then, everyone else will be coming between 3:00 PM and 7:00 PM. We will need ongoing food and drink throughout that time, say… coffee, tea, plenty of finger sandwiches, cheeses, fruit, and sweet treats. Any food leftover can go to the staff. Sometimes they need to be comforted, too." Elizabeth adds.

On the day after the viewing, the vicar has the service for close family only, inside the house, followed by the burial in the family plot.

Chapter 36

John, Elizabeth, and Robert are sitting in the library one evening after dinner, going over some plans for the future. John tells them, "There are things I need to continue working on at the law firm. In order to do this, I would like to stay in London, at the townhouse, for the time being." He continues, "Would you mind continuing to handle any affairs that need to be taken care of until I can work this out?" Elizabeth and Robert had already discussed this.

Robert tells John, "The house is yours now, John. Anything we can do to help, we would be glad to do it. Actually, Elizabeth is the expert, here," he admits, She responds, "You will be getting married in late May, so let us work around that goal point. I do not want to be underfoot for Katherine after your marriage; but I also want her to feel comfortable and acquainted with the place. Then, after she knows her way around, I am sure she will run the place properly. How does that sound? When you both move in, I will see if Katherine and I can make some time. After that, you are on your own….well, not really. We will be staying at Robert's place, in London, if you need anything," Elizabeth says.

January turns into February, and it is still cold, even into March.

Letitia has not taken the twins outside for fear they will catch cold. So, Elizabeth pays a call to see how she is doing. Her 'new mother' friend is looking somewhat better. Elizabeth is doing a little better, too. Letty talks about the Christening, explaining, "When I planned the Christening for the twins the first week in April, I was looking forward to warmer weather and sunnier skies". She laughs ruefully, "You know Robert is to be the godfather and my sister will be the twin's godmother. I also invited Mrs. Beals, who was the midwife, that night. She is excited about seeing the twins, again. When I think of what could have happened without Robert and Mrs. Beals being here…." Letty is silent for a moment. Then she resumes, "The Christening will take place, in London, at the St. Lawrence Anglican Church on Gresham Street, which was rebuilt using the designs of Sir Christopher Wren, after the fire of 1666. There will be a lot of people in attendance. That is what comes from being from a prominent, 'noble' family. My mother-in-law is delighted, of course. She told Hugh that she was buying the Christening gowns, so there was no arguing with that! Well, she spent a small fortune having them made; and she's absolutely thrilled with the babies." In a lower voice she says, "I suppose that means she will visit more often; probably stay here when she comes because she does not live close by anymore. She moved closer to her daughter when she got married, last year. Did I tell you we have chosen the names: Wesley and Denise?" Letty looks down at the two baskets with the babies and says, "Honestly, they are getting so chubby, that I would not recognize them as the same small babies from three months, ago." Elizabeth asks, "Are you getting enough sleep, Letty?" "Yes, but it is only three hours here and two hours there. I am told that they will start sleeping through the night very soon. Then, we will all get some rest," she replies. Elizabeth thinks her friend looks weary, so she decides to let Letty rest. "I must go, now, Letty. I will call again soon." She kisses Letty and the babies, "And, do not forget, if I can help with anything, please, let me do so."

The following day, Elizabeth is in town for a community committee meeting. Katherine will meet her there, after leaving work. After one of her errands, she stops in a coffee shop and sees Wrede at a table by himself, looking over some papers. Happy to see him, she goes over to say hello. He stands to greet her and gestures for her to take a seat. Knowing him as well as she does, she happily sits down. Smiling she says, "It is so good to see you. I have missed our talks. How are you enjoying retirement?" He responds, "I am not quite sure, yet. Sometimes I have nothing to do; other times I have too much." They both laugh. She asks, questioningly, "Have you taken on another position, to keep busy?" With a saddened expression, he responds, "No, not really. A few months ago, my son was injured at his job. His leg was badly broken and although it has healed, he walks with a limp; it is very stressful for him. A lot of his work is done outside, so his leg gets a little stiff, as well." He looks down, "He's a bright fellow, but I'm worried about the future for him and his family." He continues, "But why am I talking about all this to you? You have had your own sorrows recently, too. You had a very nice funeral service for your father. He was always very proud of you." Elizabeth puts her hand across the table, on top of his and thinks," *This man was like a second father*

to me, caring and courteous. There must be something I can do."
They talk for a few more minutes.

Sincerely, she says, "I am very sorry to hear this, but I am glad that you told me. Where does your son live?" Wrede tells her, "They have a small place, on the outskirts of London." Finishing her coffee, Elizabeth says, "I have a meeting, now. But, I will be in touch. It was good to see you."

Kissing him lightly on the cheek, she leaves. Thinking about this, she walks down the street and sees Katherine waiting outside the community building for her. Suddenly, an idea pops into her head. Elizabeth introduces Katherine to the ladies on the committee. Smiling at each of them, she blends in and is quickly one of them. Elizabeth understands why this woman is so good at her business and why she will be a good agent for the estate, too. Elizabeth is happy to be leaving these responsibilities in her hands. She thinks, once again, "*My brother has picked a gem!* "After the meeting, at which Katherine took notes, Elizabeth asks her, "Do you have a little more time? I have an idea that I would speak to you about." Katherine says, "Yes, I am in no particular hurry."

Chapter 37

Elizabeth takes her to tea and asks her about her position at the shipping company. Katherine explains, in broad strokes, what the job encompasses. Her brother must find someone to replace her but they are having a little trouble doing so. Elizabeth expresses, "I may have someone in mind, a man, if that is not a problem. He is intelligent, hardworking, and is used to responsibility. He was recently injured on the job. It left him with a limp. He is worried that he will be fired, soon because of this." She goes on, "He does not know anything about shipping; however, I am sure he would learn quickly. Would you and your brother be willing to talk to him, get his measure, and see if he might work out?" Katherine responds, "We certainly would! Time is getting close for the wedding; confidentially, I do not think my brother would feel comfortable working with another woman." Elizabeth says "Then, if it is all right, I will ask the man to come to your office and talk to you, both, when it is convenient." Satisfied, both women leave the tea room to make plans.

Christening day arrives. Lady Letitia was right; with about one hundred people attending the Christening ceremony, it is an unusually large event. The church is magnificent and the choir, singing for the occasion, is exquisite. It also happens to be the official church of the Lord Mayor of London; so, it is filled with nobility. Robert is looking handsome in his new three piece suit and Elizabeth has taken special care with her hair and new silk dress. People address Robert by his formal title, His Lordship, Earl of Westerbrook. Mrs. Beals sees the two of them among the crowd and moves to say hello. Realizing that Robert will be at the front of the church to participate as godfather, Elizabeth asks Mrs. Beals if she would not mind sitting with her, ostensibly, because she knows so few people here. The relief on Mrs. Beals' face is confirming. Elizabeth talks easily with her, sometimes introducing Mrs. Beals to the nobles that she meets, not always to their delight. True to Elizabeth's experience with nobles: some are well-mannered, some are condescending, and some are just oafs in expensive clothing. During the baptism, Elizabeth smiles because Robert is holding Wesley and his loud crying can be heard by the whole church; Denise accepts the water poured over her head, stoically. She thinks, *This is good practice for Robert!*

Later, when they are finally leaving the reception, Robert offers to give Mrs. Beals a ride home.

The next morning as Elizabeth and Robert are walking along the gallery to the dining room, for breakfast, Robert notices that Lord Addington's bedroom door is open. Robert asks about it. Elizabeth explains that she asked the valet to keep the door open for the dog's sake. She says, "He is lonely. He likes to go in there and lie down." As they are walking, she turns to Robert and asks, "Did I ever tell you the story about the dog?" Raising an eyebrow, Robert remarks, "The dog has a story?" "Of course!" Elizabeth begins, "Years ago, one of my father's Springer Spaniels had a litter. When they were about a year old, they began to be trained for hunting.

All of them did well, except Leo. He never seemed to take to it. As soon as he would see my father, he would run to him and want to play. Eventually, Leo never left his side. One day, when Leo was a little over two years old, my father and the dog were walking the perimeter of the estate. All at once, Leo got in front of my father and started barking and growling at something in the bushes. He even bared his teeth, something he had never done before…or since. His barking was so fierce, that a man ran out of the bushes and off the property. The fellow was probably one of those horrible highwaymen, lurking about. Who knows what would have happened to my father if Leo had not been there? Agent Wrede sent a few workers to the site to make sure the man was gone. After that, Leo became a full-fledged member of the family. That was ten years, ago." Robert nods, appreciatively. "Well, I shall remember to watch that the door is always open for him."

Within a week, Elizabeth receives a note from Ronald Taylor, indicating he and his sister would be very interested in speaking with Michael Wrede, regarding the upcoming position at the shipping company. Elizabeth is pleased. She met Michael a few times, over the years through his father, and thinks he would be extremely suitable for the job. Eventually, a plan is developed: Katherine will work with Michael in the weeks approaching the wedding. After that, he or Ronald can always contact Katherine.

Over the last several months, Robert has been in contact with scientists and physicians exchanging ideas, experiences, and thoughts about future programs. He has even written to, and is now familiar with three doctors, all of whom he came to know through his friend, Mr. Thomas Denham, in Philadelphia, Pennsylvania. He has learned of new techniques from them, and when needed, he has sent them medicines and chemicals, not readily available in the colonies.

Chapter 38

After months of preparation, John and Katherine's wedding day is upon them. John is at the manor house, getting dressed, and will leave from there. All three: John, Elizabeth, and Robert are dressed in their finest. They will take two separate coaches to the church. Since Katherine and John have residences near each other in London, they are congregates of the same parish. The wedding will be held at St Andrews Church, Kingsbury, in northwest London. The church dates back to the 12th or 13th century and is in the diocese of the Bishop of Canterbury, who will perform the wedding ceremony. Ronald will give his sister away. Robert will be best man for John, and Elizabeth will be matron-of-honor for Katherine. The young daughter of a friend of Katherine's, Julie, will be the flower girl. Guests will number well over two hundred and include a variety of people: relatives, friends, business associates, law partners, city and noble officials, including some cabinet members, and members of the 'ton. Two carriages were made available for some of the staff of Addington Manor who would also like to attend. One of John's closest friends, Lord Anthony Ashley-Cooper, offered his estate for the wedding breakfast and John gladly accepted. With the church beautifully decorated and everyone seated, Elizabeth has sent word that the bride is ready to start. The Bishop and his assistants appear on the altar; the groom and best man stand waiting. All rise as the musicians in the choir loft begin to play Pachelbel's *Canon in D Major.* Slowly, the wedding party proceeds down the long aisle. The bride looks radiant! Not a bit nervous, she walks alongside her brother, perfectly composed, as if she were created just for this moment. John cannot believe this wonderful young woman will be his wife: a thoughtful, loving, humorous, helpmate. Could a man want for more in life? When she reaches the altar, she turns, slightly, to smile at John. His heart is too full for words; his eyes tell her everything she needs to know. The Bishop of Canterbury welcomes everyone and speaks to the congregation about this auspicious occasion. Then, he asks the couple to recite their marriage vows and prays over the couple. The choir and organist perform Bach's *Jesu, Joy of Man's Desiring*, while the Bishop and the couple go into the vestry room for the signing of both Registers. Upon returning, the Bishop gives a brief homily for the bridal couple. He gives the couple a blessing and wishes them a joyful married life. The couple turns toward the congregation for a moment; they take a deep breath, and recess down the aisle, to Bach's *Brandenburg Concertos #3*. Elizabeth and Julie, the little flower girl, walk side by side behind the joyous couple. At the two double doors near the entry, the couple stops and shares a kiss before forming the receiving line. The new couple gladly receives all the warm wishes and complements that come from everyone who attended. The guests depart for the Earl of Shaftesbury's Estate, a few miles away, where the wedding breakfast will be held. Meeting old friends and greeting new ones, the smiling couple exchanges a few words to everyone before the guests are called to sit down for the special wedding breakfast. After the meal, brandy and champagne are handed to all, a toast is given to the bride and groom, in their honor. John proposes a second toast. He lifts his glass and says, "To all our loved ones, who are with us in spirit today."

The party continues until mid-afternoon, when the guests start taking their leave. John and Katherine give their sincerest thanks to the Earl and Lady Clare for their generosity.

A small, close group of family members, head for Addington Manor to change clothes and see that the carriage is correctly loaded. The group, alone in the drawing room, recount the wonderful day.

Elizabeth has told Katherine how wonderful she looks. The couple has changed into travel clothes. In two hours, the loaded carriage, with two outriders, will take them to the ship that will cross the channel. They will spend the first night in Paris. In the two months that they expect to be gone, they will travel through France, into Italy, then head north to Germany. They will be home by end of July.

Hugh and Letitia were at today's celebration and Elizabeth was happy to see that her friend is looking much better, more rested. When asked, Letitia explains, "The twins have been sleeping through the night for the last month; which means I get to do the same. At almost four months old, they are on regular schedules; the wet nurse and dry nurse can handle most everything. Every afternoon, though, I insist that in good weather we take them for a walk. At first, I tried to hide this fact from my mother-in-law, who was still 'coming to stay' from time to time. Now, I do not even bother. Maybe one day she will come with us; I do not count on it." Elizabeth says, "Well, whatever you are doing, it is working for you!"

While Katherine is upstairs changing, Ronald takes this opportunity to tell Robert and Elizabeth how grateful he is that his sister has married into such a warm, welcoming family. Also, how satisfied he is with Michael Wrede helping him at the office.

Carriage loaded, riders ready, John and Katherine say their goodbyes to everyone and board.

Elizabeth cannot help it; she starts crying, quietly. She is losing her brother and one of her best friends. Silently, Robert hands her one of his handkerchiefs. When they are truly alone, in the manor for one of only a few times, Robert turns to Elizabeth; she knows that look and she replies, "Robert, it is not even dark, yet!" With most of the servants busy, he turns and walks slowly toward Elizabeth. To her utter surprise, he scoops her up into his arms and carries her upstairs. They lock the doors. They will not be down for tea, this afternoon..

Chapter 39

A month goes by and Elizabeth continues with her activities as the agent, while Katherine is away. Robert continues his correspondence with Mr. Thomas Denham, his merchant friend who has traveled twice across the Atlantic and met Robert through mutual friends. By way of friendly conversation, Robert had asked him many questions about his voyages and life in the colonies and Mr. Denham had given Robert one of his cards, telling him to contact him, should he ever be interested in visiting. Robert had kept it all this time.

About four weeks after the wedding, the unthinkable happens. King George the First dies from a stroke, while visiting his birthplace, Osnabruck, Germany. The bells toll in London, flags are moved to half-staff, windows are draped in black. The news has spread quickly back to England to notify the Prince of Wales and Princess Caroline that they, and their family, are to be conveyed to St. James Palace, the King's official residence, by the Kings guards.

Lady Mary Wortley-Montagu is one of the first to hear the news; as she promised to do, she sends a letter notifying Elizabeth of these changes. As the day goes on, more information comes, confirming the King's death. Newspapers carry the word to all citizens. Posters go up in small villages. Elizabeth writes a brief statement, which is posted in their town.

After two days of traveling, the news catches up with John and Katherine. John makes arrangements for them to return home as quickly as possible. He sends a post to Elizabeth, telling her that he will avoid the Alps and Germany and go northwest, through France, crossing at Calais.

Two weeks later, Lady Mary sends another note to Elizabeth with confirmation that Elizabeth's name is on the list of attendants; at the coronation, Queen Caroline will have her Ladies-in-Waiting in place and ready to serve. Upon receiving this latest statement, Elizabeth hurries to find Robert.

That afternoon, Robert and Elizabeth remain sequestered in the library, asking not to be disturbed.

Robert asks Elizabeth for her thoughts. Elizabeth confesses, "Oh Robert, I guess I was always hoping it would never come to this. I cannot…I will not be separated from you, just to work for the Queen. It means that I, and my family, would incur the wrath of the royal household. I would not put anyone through that, especially after everything that has happened these last few months, I really did not even entertain such an unwonted idea." She starts to cry. Robert moves over and sits next to her and holds her.

After a few minutes, Robert says, "I have thought about this a great deal. It was only a matter of time. At some point, George the First would die and most likely, George the Second and Princess Caroline would succeed to the throne. There are many places where we could *not* go. For political reasons they include France, Spain, Germany, Portugal, Italy, and other Hanoverian provinces. So, I wonder what you think of going to the American colonies? " Elizabeth's head comes up sharply, "Robert, it is so far away, thousands of miles and it is barbaric."

Robert counters, "Here is why I think we should consider it. They speak English. We could find a developed area, where the colonists are primarily English; meaning they would have the same customs, foods, and we would still be English citizens. I could be a doctor anywhere. From what I have studied, and people I have corresponded with, I believe we could make a new life for ourselves in a place called Philadelphia. Perhaps, someday when Caroline is no longer Queen, we might want to come back? Philadelphia is growing. Yes, things would be harder for us, at first, but together, I think we could do this. Will you think about it?" Elizabeth says, "Robert, I will go anywhere with you. I have no life without you. I would like one promise from you, though. If, after King George and Queen Caroline are no longer on the throne, I wish to return to England, you will be open to the idea." Robert takes her hands in his, and says, "Yes, I promise." With heavy hearts they begin making a plan to leave their country; keeping the plan to themselves, for now.

Things must move quickly. Robert wants Elizabeth to pack three trunks of their clothing and personal effects that will be sent ahead, by ship, to Philadelphia. Robert will contact his friend, Thomas Denham, and ask him to store the trunks that will be coming. If possible, he would also like Denham to find a small house to rent, when they arrive in Philadelphia. He will meet with Ronald, in the strictest confidence, to find out about ships leaving London for Philadelphia, how often, and when to book passage. Robert hopes that seeing familiar items in their new home will soften Elizabeth's loss, even in some small way. He has told her she may send as much as she likes. To mitigate the risk of losing any of these items, they will be sent on different ships, over a period of weeks. Neither of them speaks of this where they can be overheard.

They go in to dinner with their minds and hearts full of mixed emotions. Later, that night, as if to confirm that, in the midst of all the changes, they still have a tangible constant in each other; they make love with abandon.

Chapter 40

Lady Mary Wortley-Montagu sends a note to Elizabeth, asking to see her. The following day, Elizabeth goes to Lady Mary's house, for greater secrecy. Feeling confident that Lady Mary will keep her confidences, Elizabeth tells her of their plans. Lady Mary reassures her, that if you are with someone you love, then anywhere can be home. She tells Elizabeth that, "… the Royal Coronation date is set for the 11th of October 1727, Westminster Abbey; and the King and Queen's household will be finalized by early in September. Notices to the Ladies-in-Waiting will be sent by September 1st, 1727." She adds, "You will not have much time; but it is possible to do this. If there is anything I can do to help you and Robert, please let me know."

Feeling slightly relieved at being able to unburden herself to someone who understands, Elizabeth leaves with renewed direction and impetus.

John and Katherine will be home in three days. Elizabeth and Robert talk and move about as if nothing is amiss. But, there is someone who has been watching and wondering!

Two day later, Robert and Elizabeth go to visit Ronald at his office, after hours. He has information for them about trans-Atlantic voyages: two merchant ships leave England for Philadelphia every other week taking cargo, so they can use those crossings for their trunks and personal items. There are two shipping lines that leave London and dock in Philadelphia carrying cargo and some passengers. The dates they leave port are June 29th, July 14th, July 20th, and August 21st. Robert and Elizabeth know that June 29th is too soon to be ready, and August 21st is too late to leave. They decide on July 20th, less than a month away. Ronald will contact the Black Ball Line and arrange for their reservations and passage. He tells them, "It is not unusual for passengers to have to bring their own food with them; I will find out particulars from the agent at that office. Just, be prepared."

Chapter 41

The following day, John and Katherine arrive home in the late afternoon. It is agreed that they meet in the drawing room for drinks before dinner. Nothing will be mentioned at the table; there will be plenty of travel talk to share.

Ronald and Stephen join everyone for breakfast. John has told Lewis that they would like privacy during breakfast and to please have all the carafes and serving dishes delivered at the same time. Assured that no one will interrupt them, Robert explains the situation and what he and Elizabeth have decided. He informs them of the research he started doing a few months ago, in case it came to this and why Philadelphia would be the best place for them to settle. He has some contact names already, through his medical work. Elizabeth tells them that some trunks of clothing and personal items have already been shipped. She tells John there are a few family items she would like to take, but she will show John and Katherine what they are. They can decide. Robert and Elizabeth will store their travel cases that they will take on board, at the Taylor Shipping office, so when they leave the manor, no one will suspect anything. Robert's brother will take them to London, pick up the cases, and take them to the ship. Money and Elizabeth's jewels have been sewn into the fabric of her dresses that went into different trunks. Robert will have money on him and also some in hidden pockets.

Fiona has begun to notice clothing missing, along with personal effects. Recently, some family items, meant for Elizabeth, have been removed from the manor. She suspects Elizabeth and Robert are going away; but, where, why, and for how long? Fiona feels strongly that she must talk to her mistress; she thinks they will be leaving quite soon. Fiona wants to go with them.

That evening while helping Elizabeth, and with Robert downstairs talking to John, she seizes her chance. Fiona says, "Lady Elizabeth, I could not help noticing that things are changing. Your clothing has been packed, without my help, and some of your jewelry is missing. It's not my business, but if you are in any trouble, perhaps I could help, in some way?" Fiona looks distressed. It occurs to Elizabeth that Fiona might think that she is at odds with Robert and is selling things to help her out of a bad situation. Elizabeth smiles at the sweet, loyal girl, who seems willing to keep her secret. She declares, "First of all, I thank you for your offer of help. That's very kind of you; I assure you, I am not in any real trouble." This does not mollify Fiona. It only serves to add more questions. Seeing this, Elizabeth realizes she is going to have to say a little more. "I know I can trust you…." Fiona interrupts, enthusiastically with, "Of course you can, my Lady." Then seeing Elizabeth's look, stops talking. Elizabeth continues, "Robert and I are making some changes to our lives. Instead of being one of the Ladies at court, Robert and I will be moving." She says this slowly, watching Fiona's expression for understanding. Fiona remarks, "But, will you not have to return when the Queen calls you?" At this point, Elizabeth knows she must divulge the whole story and hope she will keep it secret.

"Fiona, Robert and I are going far away, leaving the country. We will not be coming back." Stunned, Fiona sits down hard in the nearest chair. Silently, she tries to process this information. Elizabeth does not say anything, giving the girl a moment. Fiona responds, "Take me with you!" Now, it is Elizabeth's turn to be surprised, and quiet. A maid knocks and enters the room. Seeing the two women in conversation, she stops. Elizabeth says, "Hello, Betsy, could you come back in a little while?" She curtsies and leaves. Elizabeth explains, "Fiona, we are going far away, to the colonies. We are going to start a new life in a very different place. We will not have a fine home like this. We are leaving because it is our only option if Robert and I want to spend our lives together. I am sure you would not want to leave your family and England. I could talk to Lady Katherine about your staying on. She is a very nice woman." Fiona counters, "But, I have no family here. My brother is still in Ireland and can barely support his small family. I am twenty-one years old. I have been in service for eight years, now. I have enjoyed working for you. You have been kind to me; but I would not want to start over again, with another Lady. This may be the only chance I will ever get, in my whole life, to do something more. I sew very well, and I have been learning to cook. I could be helpful to you, just starting out over there. I have been saving my money, too. I would not be a burden to you. Please, just say you will think about it, and I will not ask again." Seeing her imploring expression, Elizabeth agrees to consider it. She finds she is not as immediately averse to the idea as she thought. She will think about it, carefully, so that she can answer any questions that Robert might have. This must be done by tomorrow if they are to get an extra passenger ticket. She discovers she is already planning for Fiona to come. She has surprised herself, well, not really.

Before lunch, Elizabeth asks Robert to walk around the grounds with her. Robert considers it an odd request; looking at her face, he says, "Yes, that would be nice."

On their walk, Elizabeth tells him the whole conversation with Fiona. He is not terribly surprised that she began to suspect something. She is a smart girl. After weighing the matter, he finds he does not have any real objections; Fiona can always return if she does not like it. He will find out from Ronald if there is another ticket available for one more passenger.

Ronald has checked, and the ship leaving on July 20th is full. But, the vessel leaving on July 14th has three passenger openings. Robert asks him to book those spaces. It gives them only three weeks. Ronald explains that although it is a schooner by design, it is referred to as a 'packet' sailing vessel, because it carries mail pouches back and forth across the Atlantic, in addition to cargo and passengers. Robert gives the news to Elizabeth that they will be able to leave on July 14th and Fiona can come with them, if she still wants to. Fiona is joyous and grateful beyond measure.

She has collected her savings and the next morning offers all of it to Elizabeth. She tells the girl she will not need it, yet, but to sew it into the skirt she will wear when they leave. She also tells Fiona to write to her brother, explaining where she is going, and that she will write, again, when she arrives in the colonies.

Chapter 42

The days fly by. Elizabeth has seen her friends and neighbors, only telling them that she and Robert are taking a belated honeymoon. To her closest friends, Lady Letitia and Lady Mary, she has disclosed the whole truth. Lady Letitia is sorrowful at losing her. Lady Mary is more understanding. Both will miss her sorely. She promises to write when she arrives.

The morning of July 14th arrives. They have breakfast with everyone. Stephen has brought the coach to take them to London, pick up their cases at the office, and then go to the dock at Gravesend, a few miles south of London. Robert notices that Fiona has been helpful and has kept their secret.

In the coach, Elizabeth starts to cry. Robert gives her a handkerchief and puts his arm around her. Fiona is all smiles. At the wharf, the coachman unloads all their cases and brings them on board, while Elizabeth and Robert give goodbye hugs. Stephen tips his hat to Fiona and wishes her well. They go aboard and get their first look at where they will be for the next several weeks. All quarters are very close; but those who have paid full fare have slightly more personal space. They also have access to what is called, the saloon, which is a ship's lounge area, on the middle deck. There, they can relax, read, and eat whatever food they have brought with them. A crewman is showing the passengers their designated sleeping quarters and necessary areas of the ship. He explains the system of water rationing and where they are permitted on the open deck. There are sixteen crewmen; all are busy getting the ship ready to up-anchor in two hours.

Below deck, Elizabeth is going through her case. Robert notices and asks, "Are you looking for something, in particular?" She says, "As a parting gift, Lady Mary W.M. gave me a journal, a small writing plate, and a beautiful pen and ink set. She thought it would help take my mind off what might be a long and boring journey. Also, she wants to know about everything in my first letter, after we arrive. So, I thought I would get ready, in case there was anything to write about." Fiona, who has quarters nearby, asks Elizabeth, "My Lady, is there anything you need that I can help with?" Elizabeth talks to her quietly. "Please, call us Elizabeth and Robert, now. You no longer work for us; we are traveling together. And, your time is your own. From now on, we will help each other, as people would normally do who care about each other." For the first time in her life, Fiona reaches out and hugs Elizabeth. All three have hidden their valuables, so, they do not mind going up to the saloon deck for a while.

One of the women, Mrs. Smith, who is traveling with her grown daughter, smiles and engages them in conversation as soon as they enter the room. A person of many questions for Elizabeth, she also seems to be someone who knows a lot about what goes on, too. She tells them there are fifteen passengers and five people who are one deck below. You probably will not see much of them, anyway. Elizabeth asks her why? Mrs. Smith replies, "Because they have not paid their full fair. They are indentured servants. When they arrive, businessmen or sponsors will bid on them… saying how much they will be pay for their labor, and how many years they will have to work to repay their sponsors for their passage. My daughter and I have traveled extensively, and we have seen this before. But we are seeing fewer and fewer servants, anymore. I think more people in the southern colonies are buying a greater number of slaves, instead. It makes more sense: they never leave, and you do not have to pay them!" Mrs. Smith finishes drolly. Not willing to make an enemy so quickly, Elizabeth says nothing.

Everyone feels the ship give a small lurch; realizing that the ship is underway, the passengers go up on the deck and watch as the harbor slowly moves away, and with it, England. Elizabeth stands by the railing, watching until it is too dark to see. Robert has brought her cloak out and stands close behind her. A tall, lanky man, in his early thirties, accompanied by a boy of about ten, stands further down the railing, sorrowfully, quietly watching, as well. He and his son will have something to eat below deck. Exhausted, most of the passengers sleep tolerably.

Chapter 43

JOURNAL: July 15th, 1727 *The London Hope,* London, England to Philadelphia, Pennsylvania

I received a wonderful writing set from Lady Mary W.M. I am going to write about our experiences aboard the schooner, crossing the Atlantic. Let me explain a little about the ship, also called a packet ship; because it carries 'packets' of mail trans-Atlantic. It may also carry merchant goods, expensive articles, and large quantities of banking currency, from England to colonial banks. For that reason, it is sometimes the target of pirate vessels. Nothing to do about that, now! The schooner has three large masts, making it fast and agile. I hope it is fast enough!

Yesterday, I met Mrs. Smith, who is traveling with her daughter and knows everything about anything! Probably because she has no problem asking everyone questions, most of which are none of her business. I like to spend time out on deck. The air is cooling and smells fresh…and Mrs. Smith does not usually go up there. Fiona is doing well.

July 16th, 1727

The ship is going northwest to the Trade Winds. We will pass the Canary Islands.

A schedule of moving about seems to be emerging among the passengers. A man, woman, and young daughter are sometimes seen at early meals. Their family name is Descantes. She will often stay in the saloon after her meal, working on her knitting. After speaking on several occasions, the wife divulges that they are leaving France because they are protestant Huguenots, and the French government has become increasingly hostile toward that religion. Three other couples, who have married without the family's permission are leaving for greater opportunities. I have seen this happen more often, in the last ten years. A generation ago, a daughter married whoever her father picked, sometimes sight unseen. Two merchants are returning to the colonies after contracting with business firms in London. The men were very careful not to mention the nature of their cargo. A few others are seen, only in passing; I do not know their names. Fiona has stayed near Robert and me. Most people are eating the food they brought because the meat that is served is very salty. Robert hopes we will not lose any time in the voyage. He thinks some people will run out of food. Ships can be delayed three or four weeks due to the weather and the seas. The same casks that are now holding our drinking water have also been used to hold tobacco leaves on a prior voyage; our drinking water tastes like tobacco.

July 19th, 1727

Each night, after dinner, Robert and I go up to the deck and get some fresh air. We have learned that the man with the boy is Jack Turner and his son is Tomas, or Tom, as he is called. He and Robert have begun to say a few words to each other. He learned that Jack's wife died of smallpox two years ago. It seems the only way he could afford to start life over was to come as an indentured servant. He will have to work for a man for ten years and because he brought his son, he will add another four years to his indenture. He is willing to do that, rather than leave England without his son.

Mrs. Smith was talking to Fiona when she misspoke and referred to me as Lady Elizabeth. Immediately, Mrs. Smith noticed it and asked if Robert and I were of the nobility. Fiona said she did not know what to do, so she just excused herself, and left. The story we are giving is that we have relatives living in the colonies and we are visiting them. I am glad we sent all those trunks with our things ahead of us.

July 21st, 1727

Last evening, I awoke during the night thinking that something was different. I realized that the ship was not moving. At breakfast, we got word that we had lost the wind. The sails were down; and all we can do is wait for the wind or weather to change. We were told we could each have only one cup of water per day.

July 23rd, 1727

Two days later, and the sea was still calm; but we had a surprise after lunch. Two of the passengers are violinists. Mr. Smithson and Mr. Travest, are traveling together to join a budding orchestra in Philadelphia. They brought up chairs and their music stands and gave a concert as we sat on the deck. Even the crew enjoyed it. What a wonderful little duo they were!

July 24th, 1727

We were having breakfast when the wind started! What a relief it was to see the sails billow out and the crew scurrying about. We were on our way, again.

The Trade Winds began to carry us a good distance; all was well for a while. Some passengers began to complain about the heavily salted meat and food. The one meal a day that the ship offers is becoming too much for people's stomachs. Add to that the close quarters of others around who are less tolerant, and tempers start to flare.

The three of us spent most of our time 'up top', as they say.

July 27th, 1727

Two days of rain. We were all inside, together. I suspect someone came on board with lice; everyone seems to be scratching!

Besides my journal, I brought a small book in my travel case; I am frequently reading it.

August 5th, 1727

I have not had a chance to write because terrible things have happened. On July 29ᵗʰ, the rain intensified and turned into a gale force storm. You cannot imagine the battering this little ship endured. Everyone hunkered down. It was dangerous enough to be inside; but no one dared to open the door to go out, lest they be blown overboard. People prayed, cried, and worried if we would make it through the storm alive. Everyone was anxious.

People stayed in their bunks, otherwise they would get knocked down. Port holes were closed, so the passenger's area, below deck, became very dark except for a single oil lamp which swung back and forth as the ship rolled. No meals were served; all crewmembers were at their stations trying to hold the ship steady. During that time, passengers had to eat whatever they brought with them. That is if they wanted to eat, at all! I am told the bow, or front of the ship, must enter the wave straight-on, or else the waves will broadside the ship, and we will surely capsize. This is no small feat; it took at least two men to hold the wheel steady, under such conditions. Water, food, and slop buckets spilled over, and the stench was overpowering. Items fell off the walls, furniture moved across the room, plowing into things. Passengers vomited. I did not feel very well, either. This continued for almost three days.

When the storm ended and the damage surveyed, we were missing one crewman, another had a broken arm, one of the passengers suffered serious injuries, and Jack Turner had a head injury. Robert has been working, almost constantly, with the injured and sick; the Captain and crew are now trying to fix the sails that were torn. It is assumed that the missing crewman went overboard. Robert created a work detail. All the able-bodied passengers were put to work with brooms, brushes, and sea water, cleaning the deck. They stayed topside while all passenger quarters and saloon were cleaned and cleared of broken objects. At first Mrs. Smith thought she should not be involved in the work; but she was *persuaded* to help out. After all was done, a few women came up with an idea to make a bathing area. Taking an empty barrel, sea water was used to fill it on the deck. Ropes hung bedding, cloaks, nightshirts…anything that could be found, was used to make a privacy area for those who wanted to bathe. At first, the men were shocked and ridiculed the idea; after a while, when the ladies had gone to their quarters, the men took turns. The water was very cold, and people did not take much time, but it felt like a piece of heaven. Later, the same barrel was refilled, and each person used it to wash their soiled clothing. By dinner, passengers were tired and thankful.

August 7th, 1727

Last night I had my first good night's rest in about three weeks; but I felt ill, again, in the morning. Some passengers are still ill from the storm. Robert has been keeping an eye on Jack. He thinks he may have a concussion. He also made a splint for the sailor's arm. And Mr. Whitcombe, James, I think is his name, was badly injured when the heavy dining table struck him, knocking him to the floor. He probably has internal bleeding because areas of him are black and blue and very painful. We have also lost provisions. The Captain has started rationing supplies and food.

August 9th, 1727

Robert spent the day tending to Mr. Whitcombe. His side and back have turned a purple color and he is in great pain. Robert has given him some laudanum. He says there is nothing to be done for him, under these conditions.

August 10th, 1727

Mr. Whitcombe passed away during the night. The Captain will preside over a burial at sea service. All crewmembers not on duty, along with passengers, are expected to be present and on deck during the service. It is considered a matter of respect.

August 11th, 1727

In about two weeks, we will be in Philadelphia. Jack Turner still gets terrible headaches when he tries to sit up and gets dizzy when he looks around. He now has a cloth around his eyes, to keep him from moving about. Tom has been staying at his father's side, talking to him. Fiona brings him soup, trying to get him to eat something. I see Tom sitting next to her; she puts her arm around the boy. They seem to need each other.

We will pick up the Gulf Stream in a couple of days. Then, all we have to worry about will be pirates, who wait for ships heading to the colonies. I am trying to see if Tom has any more food in their baggage. I will make sure that he gets some of ours.

One of the three other indentured servants is not sure she will have anyone to pay her fare once the ship reaches Philadelphia. Mrs. Smith has told me that, unless their voyage fare is paid completely, the person is not allowed to leave the ship. I also learned that if a family member or spouse dies during the voyage, and the ship is more than halfway across the Atlantic, the fare must be paid or the remaining family member is required to take on their indentured time, too.

I will talk to Robert, when he has a few minutes, about Jack and his son. I am wondering if he asked Jack what kind of trade work he does?

August 13th, 1727

The wind is with us and we are making good time. We cannot get there too soon, for me!

August 15th, 1727

We are still rationing food and water. If there are no more storms or pirates, we will stop rationing tomorrow.

August 16th, 1727.

While we were up on deck, last night, Robert and I spoke privately about Jack and Tom.

Robert told me that Jack is healing, slowly, but it is best not for him to move around and let his skull mend. He explained that no businessman will want to indenture him since he cannot work. He will be left on board; instead, they may take the boy. Under these circumstances, Jack will be free to leave the ship; because Tom has become indentured and will have to work his father's number of indentured years, too. Also, it is very possible that Jack and Tom will never see each other, again. Families separated like this are often sold again, to different purchasers. Sometimes, family members never find each other." I am determined that we cannot let this happen. After lunch Robert said, "If you agree, I would like to pay for the fares of both Jack and Tom." I told him, "Of course, I agree. We shall adjust our expenses, accordingly." Robert told me, "Tomorrow, I will speak to the Captain about paying their fares and tell him I would like a written statement stating the details, names of all, amounts, and date. It would be signed by all of us, so that there is no mistake, later on." I was, in agreement and thought to myself, *"I am so grateful to have a husband with a generous spirit."*

August 17th, 1727

Robert has learned that Jack's trade is a Leatherman. He has never seen a man cry before; he was pretty sure that Jack was fighting back tears as he signed the indenture release form.

August 24th, 1727

With lighter hearts, passengers begin to collect and pack their items.

Tomorrow, our small ship will dock in Philadelphia. For all our troubles, we did avoid one big problem; no one got smallpox. The port authorities will allow us to disembark. I cannot wait!

August 25th, 1727

At nine, in the morning, the crewman up in the crow's nest yells, "Land ho!" All the passengers move to the nearest porthole for a faint view of the coastline. Quickly finishing their breakfast, several of them go upstairs and outside for a better view. Since it will take another several hours before the ship has completed its journey up the Delaware River and is docked and anchored, Robert, Jack, and I take the opportunity to meet in the Captain's quarters, sign the documents and pay the fares in full, for Jack and Tom.

The voyage is finally over. Everyone is happier than they could have imagined.

I must stop writing, now. Our trip across the Atlantic has been an exhausting and harrowing six weeks. So, here ends my journal. And our start in a new world begins.

Chapter 44

Robert has the address of the house that we have rented through Mr. Denham. Hiring a larger coach, the five of us have our bags and cases loaded and the coachman drives to our next home. It is at the end of town, nicely furnished, with seven rooms. A maid has been employed to see that the beds and rooms are ready. A cook will come with an informal supper, bread, and a bottle of wine. Denham could not be absolutely sure of the arrival date or time. I will organize what needs to be done. Even though I am not on the ship anymore, I am still a little seasick.

Before anything, I must write to Letty, Lady Mary W.M., and Robert's brother, Stephen, to let everyone know that we arrived safely and tell them about the 'interesting' voyage; we are now settled in Philadelphia, Pennsylvania. Fiona will write to her brother, also.

Tomorrow, we will find our way around the neighborhood. Jack and Tom have a nice size bedroom, in the back of the house. Belongings are carried to appropriate rooms. In the hallway are the trunks that were sent ahead. There are beautiful, well-kept flower and vegetable gardens, an outdoor sitting area, and a sloping space, further back, with an unobstructed view of the river. We will wash up and in one hour, gather for tea in the front room. Robert is glad to hear that Jack's headaches are almost gone and his double vision has disappeared, completely.

Tomorrow, Robert will go to see Mr. Thomas Denham, Jack will inquire about any leather-working positions. Fiona will sort out the trunks and put our things away. For the time being, the maid and the cook, Mrs. Pelham will continue with their work, here.

Robert has learned that Mr. Denham is sick from pleurisy; so his solicitor confirmed the rental paperwork is all in order and has been paid for the next eight months. After signing two copies of the agreement and keeping one, Robert asks the solicitor to send regards to Mr. Denham for improved health. While walking home, Robert noticed a small shop that sells sweet treats and decided to bring some home for everyone.

That evening, after dinner, Jack tells everyone that he was offered a job at the leather shop. He explains that most of the work done is for gentlemen who own horses and carriages; but the shop owner also needs someone who can make boots and shoes, belts, buckets, harnesses, saddles, pouches, and personal effects. Jack told them the idea was a great way to make his business bigger. He will start in two days. He has also found a smaller place, above a store, with two bedrooms, where he and Tom can live. It is within walking distance to his job and our house. He is so grateful and has told us that, "… should we need help with anything, I am more than willing lend a hand." I was thinking, *"Robert does not have much experience building or repairing things, so, it may be that one day Robert will have to learn from Jack."*

In any case, Robert brought out the treats and everyone celebrated.

Fiona said she will help Jack and Tom gather their things together when they are ready to move. She and Jack like to go walking after dinner. The summer weather here is warmer than London.

Fiona has begun chatting with Mrs. Pelham each day when she brings the meals. Fiona has asked the cook for instructions in meal preparation and buying fresh produce. Mrs. Pelham, who believes she is over worked anyway, is happy to see the possibility of an end to cooking for this household. She has mentioned loudly enough, that she was told it would be for only two people. Robert pays her handsomely for the extra work; but she likes to complain and be appreciated.

Robert and Elizabeth are sitting in the drawing room, having tea, and enjoying their own company, when there is a knock on their door. Upon opening the door, Elizabeth looks quizzically at a face she has seen before. The young man is certain he knows this lady; but is at a loss as to where. He says, "Excuse me. I was looking for the residence of a Doctor Robert Barnett. Does he live here?" Elizabeth responds, "Have we not met before?" She continues, "You look very much like someone I met in London, at a print shop." He says, "Oh my word! You are Lady Elizabeth of Addington Manor. I printed posters and signs for you, a while ago." As Robert comes to the door, Elizabeth turns to the young man and says, "I only know you as 'Ben'." He says, "That is right. My name is Ben Franklin. I actually live here, in Philadelphia. I worked with Mr. Denham." Robert tells him to come in and sit down. Elizabeth pours a cup of tea for him. Ben says, "I have some sad news. My employer and wonderful friend, Thomas Denham passed away yesterday afternoon, from the pleurisy." He continues, "We lived together, over the store. In fact, we both had pleurisy. I got over it. He was like a father to me; taught me so much about business, life, and how to be a good person. You see, he was a Quaker; he had dignity, integrity, and was efficient with his money. His executors will contact you, soon. But, I wanted to tell you, myself, because, from your correspondences, he told me so much about you. I feel I almost know you." Elizabeth can see this twenty-one year old young man is more emotional that he wants to let on. She says, "I am very sorry," and asks him, "What will you do?" He tells her, "They will sell the store and I will lose my job. But, I know several people in this town; I will see what happens." He continues, "I still cannot believe that you are someone I met in London. How amazing! " "About that," Robert joins in, "I....or...we would appreciate it if you did not use our titles or refer to our living in London." Robert explains why. Ben has heard many similar stories; assures them most people in the colonies would rather not address anyone with a title. He tells them that one of the ways some colonists, wishing to preserve a feeling of 'rank,' will do it by dressing in splendid clothes. Maybe you have noticed, but people in the colonies do, on occasion, dress in a genteel manner, but nothing like you see at the King's court. Life here is less formal for most of us. Well, I am sorry to have kept you. Thank you for the tea. It was delightful; I must go now." They all stand. Looking at Elizabeth, he takes her hand carefully, and bowing slightly over it, expresses sincerely, "I cannot tell you how good it is to see you. I hope I will have the pleasure again, soon, under better circumstances. Thank you."

After he leaves, Robert and Elizabeth turn to look at one another. Smiling, he asks, "Is there anything I should know?" Returning the humor, she remarks, "If I thought there was something you should know, I *might* tell you." She moves quickly, but does not escape his outstretched arm. Turning her slowly, he gently pulls her to him. She raises her face to meet his lips coming down on hers, with possession, hunger, and love. It will be an early night for them.

To My Readers

These parts of the story were true

King George the First (1660-1727) was a foreign born King of England who spoke little English, rarely attended cabinet meetings, and died of a stroke while visiting his birthplace, in Germany.

Lady Mary Wortley-Montagu (1689-1762) traveled to the Ottoman Empire with her husband, learned about vaccinating against smallpox and brought this procedure back to England, saving thousands of lives.

Caroline, Princess of Wales, had willing prisoners inoculated against smallpox to see if they would survive. All of them did.

Benjamin Franklin (1706-1790) was in London from 1724 to 1726, working in a print shop; he later worked with Thomas Denham, in Philadelphia.

Childbed Fever, the cause of death to many women after giving birth to a healthy child, was facilitated by doctors, who neither washed their hands nor their implements before assisting with the delivery.

Passengers who came to the colonies as indentured servants had contracted with another party to pay the cost of their voyage; in return, they would work for a specific number of years as repayment.

Thomas Denham (?-1727) was an esteemed Quaker merchant and beloved mentor to Ben Franklin, employing him as clerk and bookkeeper in his shop, until 1727, when Denham died from pleurisy.

Packet schooners were small, three-mast sailing vessels that regularly brought mail and large amounts of currencies from banks in England to the colonies and back. They were known targets for pirates.

The Churches mentioned: St Lawrence Jewry Anglican Church is the official church of the Lord Mayor of London and St. Andrews Church, Kingsbury, the diocese of the Bishop of Canterbury, are actual churches in London, England.

The English drank lots of coffee before tea was imported.

*Thank You for your patronage.
I hope you enjoyed the story.*

www.ingramcontent.com/pod-product-compliance
Lightning Source LLC
Chambersburg PA
CBHW051804050726
47598CB00006B/2415